S0-FAH-408

## Praise for Michael Modzelewski's

# Wild Life

"Michael Modzelewski's writing is as good as it gets!"
~Pat Conroy, author of *The Prince of Tides* and *The Great Santini*

"A fast-paced page turner in which a Cosmo Bachelor and naturalist, fresh from Alaska, dates and studies a wide range of women as if they are wildlife. The New York nights are as luminous as the Northern Lights. It's wonderful!"
~Amy Tan, author of *The Joy Luck Club*

"An explorer returns from the wilds to find himself suddenly famous, a Cosmo Bachelor with women clamoring after him. Setting out to solve the mystery of what women really want, he is led on a journey of discovery, unlike anything encountered in the wilds. Based on a true story, *WILD LIFE* is a fun read, full of adventure, sex, hilarity, but it's also more. Ultimately, it's about the search for love and meaning in the wilderness known as modern life." ~Cassandra King, author of *The Sunday Wife*, and *Queen of Broken Hearts*

"*Tom Jones* meets *Brigitte Jone's Diary* in Modzelewski's *WILD LIFE*. This witty roman 'a clef (based on the author's own experiences) contrasts lilting descriptions of the Alaskan wilds with tales of urban mating rituals, as one man attempts to find true love. It's quite a ride."
~Barbara Szerlip, author of *THE UGLIEST WOMAN IN THE WORLD and other histories*

"Michael Modzelewski is what I call a 'WOW!' He is a Master Incarnate on his last pass through this world. What he knows he shares beautifully and brilliantly in his writing!"
~Carmen Harra, author of *Everyday Karma*

"Girls, if you want to know how guys think, read this book. Guys, if you want more dates, be like Mike. "
~Juliann Matson, Life Coach

"Oh my God. What did I raise..."
~The author's mother

"A Cosmo-girl must read! After my boyfriend read *WILD LIFE* we had the greatest weekend of sex ever! Thank you, Michael."
~Lulu, the author's agent

Dear Reader,

Imagine a dream in which the Master of the Universe says to a young man: "Here is a female candy store. Walk in. The door is open. Enjoy as many different colored and flavored sweets as you want, for as long as you want. The lids are off all the jars—help yourself to all the goodies." Well, for this man, that dream came true, in the boom-boom 1990's, when I was picked by *Cosmopolitan Magazine* as a "Bachelor of The Month."

I lived every man's fantasy, receiving thousands of letters from women around the world, frilly lingerie, naked pictures, a plethora of flower bouquets, books, more mix tapes than I could count, and many invitations making it abundantly clear that if we met in person, there would be a "happy ending" on the first date, right out of the gate. What human animal with a pair of testicles and a will to live could possibly say "No?"

My literary agent, at the time, said: "My god, man, Sigmund Freud asked, 'What do women really want?' You have a golden opportunity to find out! Whatever you do -- take notes."

I did (copiously), and the book you now hold in your hands (thank you) describes the wild sex, surreal hilarity, mystical guidance from an Alaskan totem goddess, a black eye, and the deep wisdom I learned from an amazing assortment of what is the very best of this world: women.

Buckle-up, open your mind -- and enjoy the ride.

Gratefully,
Michael Modzelewski
www.YouTube.com/AdventureM
www.Twitter.com/MikeModzelewski
AdventureM@aol.com

# WILD LIFE

To the Epperson Family

Keep It Wild!

MICHAEL MODZELEWSKI

Michael Modzelewski

My life as a Cosmo Bachelor with some names and locations changed to protect the not so innocent.

CORVALLIS PRESS

WILD LIFE



I wrote this book to share my adventures as a Cosmo Bachelor. Being a gentleman, I changed names and locations to protect the not so innocent along with the innocent. 80% of the story really happened; 20% has been invented for dramatic purposes and narrative flow. As the Nobel laureate William Faulkner wrote, "Fact and truth really don't have much to do with each other." Call it a work of faction.

Cover Design by Mona Weiss (facebook.com/monaweissfans)
Author Photo by Hannah Copely

Printed in the United States of America

First Edition
First Printing, 2012

Printed ISBN: 978-0-9832568-7-8
eBook ISBN: 978-0-9832568-8-5

Corvallis Press, Publisher
630 NW Hickory Str., Ste. 120
Albany, OR 97321
www.corvallispress.com

# Dedication

To Paula

"The Church says: The body is a sin.
Science says: The body is a machine.
Advertising says: The body is a business.
The body says: I am a fiesta."

~Eduardo Galeano

# WILD LIFE

# 1

# Rip Van Winkle Wakes Up

I couldn't breathe. After living alone in the Alaskan wilderness I was now stuffed inside a 757 airplane en route to New York City. Head down and eyes shut, I was hyper-alert and losing it. Surrounded by two hundred people and hurtling along at five hundred miles per hour without being able to see ahead, each *bing-bong* seatbelt signal struck my nerves like an electric shock. Desperate to ground myself I raised the window shield, but my view was blocked by a wide metallic wing.

I was on the edge of panic when I heard a female voice ask, "Chicken or beef?"

I nodded anxiously.

"Which one?" an attractive blonde flight attendant asked.

I gasped, as if seeing a woman for the very first time, stunned and intoxicated by her beauty. My mouth opened. "Boof."

The flight attendant passed me a tray. "Lower your tray table, please."

Direction, any direction, was welcome—crucial—at this point.

She smiled and shoved the cart toward the next row. I hadn't eaten a meal that I hadn't killed and cooked myself in five years. I warily peeled back the aluminum foil of the box she'd given me and stared wide-eyed at the steaming beef and vegetables.

It seemed like an endless procession of flight attendants interrupted me as I ate. Smiling, staring, leaning toward me saying, "Anything you need? Anything at all—just press my button!"

A male flight attendant, Robbie, sashayed down the aisle in an apron and stopped…hovering. "Milk does a body good, but DAMN, how much have youuu been drinking?"

I stared at my cup of water thinking, damn, what a friendly airline.

Robbie winked, opened an overhead bin and pulled down a pillow and blanket. "Sweet dreams, babe," he said. I gave him my tray and slowly placed the pillow behind my neck baffled by all the attention.

The man who filled the two seats next to me snorted. He reached up and mashed a fat forefinger against the call button. The beautiful blonde returned. "Hey!" the red-faced man said, "What about ME? What's HE got that I don't?"

"He's still breathing." She reached down and released the seat belt that was nearly cutting the man in two. She dug her hand into her apron and pulled out an extender and clicked it into place.

"AHHH!" the man exhaled grinning. The woman rolled her eyes and turned her attention to another passenger.

I watched a young woman in the row across the aisle get up, pen in hand. She walked forward to the galley and flipped back the curtain separating it from the coach section.

She imitated the flight attendants' strut back down the aisle and handed me a napkin served with a smile.

As she returned to her seat, I stared at the napkin with her phone number and name, Brandi. A perfectly-formed purple heart dotted the i.

*WHAT THE HELL IS GOING ON?*

I tucked the napkin into my jeans pocket and closed my eyes, retreating back to what I knew to be reality. Fast asleep… I saw a bald eagle soaring effortlessly over an azure ocean with irregular shaped islands set in the water like jade jewels. Snow capped mountains scraped the sky and narrow fjords were splashed by silver plumed waterfalls. Massive glaciers glittered sapphire blue while icebergs as big as houses cracked off the glacier faces and crashed into the sea with thunderous roars. The eagle's wings wavered in the wind as it scanned the sprawling scene below. The eagle tucked its wings and arrowed down...

The plane bounced hard as it hit the runway. I was jolted awake thrashing around in my seat. I opened my mouth to apologize to the big man next to me, but thought better of trying to talk.

With the other passengers, I slid through a tunnel of flight attendants standing at attention. I was bathed in "Bye-byes!" and blinded by white teeth and lip-gloss.

Brandi held her thumb and little finger alongside her ear. "Call me?"

Walking out into the LaGuardia Airport concourse my legs didn't work right. I was used to bounding with a spring in my step over rugged trails bedded with evergreen needles that had trickled down in the forest over thousands of years. Now on the hard floor my leg muscles were locking up and I was rolling sideways more than moving forward. Honed to super-sensitivity in the wilderness all of my senses now felt assaulted by the crass billboards, shrill announcements, and pushy people.

I ducked into a stall in the Men's room and slammed down the door-latch trying to separate and absorb one sensation at a time. But the layers all came too fast, jangled and entangled. Breathing hard I braced both hands against the cold metal walls to steady myself.

After using the toilet, I couldn't find the handle. Searching for a way to flush, the toilet roared, the water whirling away suddenly on its own. I jumped back. After having peed for what seemed a lifetime in the woods and on open beaches, I waved a hand back and forth over the porcelain bowl. *What's happening? I remember all this—but it wasn't like THIS!* The haunted toilet roared again.

Back on the concourse, I found my way to Baggage Claim. While pulling my duffels from the luggage carousel, two young women stared. They whispered back and forth, bathing me with the glow of their smiles.

*I know what it is. I've entered some sort of bizarro world like in the comic books where everything is opposite. Before Alaska, women didn't even look my way.*

It was early evening outside the airport. A woman waved a bejeweled hand from a curbside cab and called my name. *Must be Liz Kingsley, the literary agent.* Tossing my bags into the open trunk, I saw even more women pointing and smiling. I slid into the cab stunned and confused.

After introducing herself and shaking my hand, Liz leaned forward toward the driver and commanded, "The Four Seasons." Originally from Texas, she was big-boned and bosomy with sky blue eyes and fire-engine red nails. She turned to me in the back seat of the cab. "Thought we'd talk over dinner—that is, if you can talk," she said, patting my knee. "How *is* your voice? You sounded terrible over the phone, but poor dear, who wouldn't be tongue-tied being all alone for so long!"

As the driver sped and swerved through New York traffic, I grabbed the edge of the seat in a white-knuckled grip like a trapped animal. When the cab was finally halted by gridlock in Times Square, I frantically rolled the window down to gulp some air and did a double-take.

On a billboard towering above the street was my picture, the one I'd sent Liz from Alaska for my book jacket, blown up sky high with the caption: FOREVER WILD! MEET COSMOPOLITAN MAGAZINE'S BACHELOR! Incredulous, I turned to Liz.

She chuckled and tugged playfully on the sleeve of my coat. "You're wearing the same parka as in the picture! I was hoping we'd pass this way…everything has happened so fast," Liz said as she snapped her fingers. "As it does when a book is good. And your picture! I was *so* impressed I messengered it over to my good friend, Helen Gurley Brown, International Editor for *Cosmopolitan*, and hells-bells… not only are you Mr. October, but I squeezed a solid advance out of a publisher for your Alaska book. Plus we've got Disney Pictures sniffin' around."

I took a deep breath and protested, "I haff no idee how ta be a *Bacheelur of tha Mon…or Yeer.* I wan no parr a it." I growled, struggling to string words together and suddenly feeling overwhelmed and exhausted.

Liz stroked my arm. "Now you won't have to do anything you don't want to. You'll get some letters and you can either answer them or not," she purred. "But being in *Cosmopolitan* is publicity you can't buy and will bump book sales through the roof. *Cosmo* is not just any magazine..."

She then reeled off the demographics; best-selling, young women's magazine in the U.S. with eighteen million readers a month and printed in thirty-four languages with distribution in more than a hundred countries worldwide.

"Michael, luv, you may have lived all by your lonesome in Alaska, but you are now what's referred to in the Biz as a mainstream situation. As we say in Texas, *you are hotter than the hinges on the gates of hell.* You're every woman's fantasy, a hunk with a brain and a sensitive soul. Saving that seal from the jaws of death and then how she ended-up sleeping in bed with you, Honey that's enough to melt any girl's heart! You jus' leave everything to lil'ole Liz. I'm gonna make you a *Staahr!*" The cab stopped in front of The Four Seasons.

Inside the posh restaurant, I was instantly forgiven by the maître d' for my lumberjack shirt and authentically ripped and distressed jeans as he cooed, "Ah, it is Mr. Bachelor!"

For dinner I ate a lot of fancy food and then signed a stack of contracts. As we walked out of the restaurant I was reeling from culture-shock, tiramisu, and the fast track Liz had placed me on. She hailed a cab with an efficient wave-whistle maneuver and pushed me into it. As the cab screeched to a halt in front of my old apartment building, I thanked her for everything, still feeling dazed and disoriented.

"There. I just put you on speed-dial," Liz said waving a tiny cell phone. "Better get one of these; they're faboo."

I nodded. *Faboo?*

"Wait," she continued. "You need this more than me..." She thumbed the gold clasps on her Coach briefcase and pulled out a huge eagle feather. "It was in with the manuscript package." I stumbled out of the cab holding the feather in front of me like a protective shield. I staggered up the stairs with my duffel bags to my old apartment on the third floor.

Inside, I walked past a towering stack of mail and a note from the sublet. I collapsed on the shabby green couch and looked around. Nothing had changed. The same grad student no-style-all-function furniture, books filling the raw wood and cinder block shelves, and a giant map of Alaska pinned to the wall above the couch. A cat jumped up into my lap.

"CHARLIE!" I hugged the cat and set him down. Walking around the apartment, I flicked a switch on the wall and the lights came on. After living without electricity for so long I flicked the switch again and again. *Everything so quick and easy.* I turned on the TV. The pictures appeared bright and painful, the pace manic, the commercials unbelievably inane. Channel surfing to help resurrect my speech. I attempted to mimic aloud the choice words of characters on various shows and movies.

First up was the comedian, Larry the Cable Guy. I struggled to repeat the simpleton's tag line, "*Git 'er done!*"

Next was Oprah seated on a couch. She raised her arms and shouted, "You go, girlfriend!" I gave it my best shot.

Then a naked woman gave *The Sopranos'* Paulie Walnuts a lap dance. After the woman stood up in all her glory, following Paulie's lead I stabbed the air with a pinkie finger and murmured, "Bada bing?"

Gathering momentum now, I listened to an ESPN Sports Center anchor describe a basketball player's jump shot as *a buzzer beater that won the game, as cool as the other side of the pillow,*" which I repeated perfectly.

On a roll now, I eagerly clicked onward stopping on a love scene from *It's A Wonderful Life.* I didn't even try to imitate the rapid-fire heartfelt eruption from Jimmy Stewart to Donna Reed. I could only gape at it open-mouthed feeling totally inadequate to the task. Wearily, I snapped off the TV.

As the sun rose I shuffled off to bed.

# 2

# Mission Control

I awoke mid-afternoon the next day. Walking to the bathroom I ran a hand over shelved biology textbooks and saw flashes of my past. I turned on the shower, stepped in and didn't move for an hour, luxuriating under the endless flow of hot water. *Man's greatest invention.* I washed over and over, sloughing off the residue of Alaskan dirt until the water finally ran clear. Before stepping out of the shower I reached down to the drain guard to remove a pinch of pine needles.

I made coffee that the sublet had left behind and turned on the television news and learned that it was Saturday. *So, the days have names again.* Sipping the fresh brew, I eyed the stack of mail on the side table by the door. Alongside the letters was a handwritten note: *Welcome back! There are some packages for you at Rathbone's house. —Ralph*

I dressed in vaguely familiar clothes I had left behind that hung loose now. *Had I really been THAT fat?* I picked up a digital wrist watch from a tray atop a chest of drawers. I laid it across my wrist then put it down. *Not ready to be rushed yet . . .*

I saw myself waking up on another morning five years before. Overweight with stooped posture and a waxen pallor. I shuffled slowly across the messy bedroom. The floor was littered with half-read books, greasy pizza boxes, and heaps of dirty clothes. The phone rang and I answered it: "*Michael, it's now Valentine's Day, but I'm sure that's news to you. I can't take it anymore! You don't know how to make a woman happy and never will. You love those damn PEAS more than me! I deserve way better. Goodbye forever, Michael!*" Click. Susie hung up on me. I dropped the phone, slumped over more and erupted into a ferocious coughing fit. Once it had stopped, I lit a cigarette and walked smoking into the shower.

That past morning I went out into a frigid, gray day. I lit another cigarette on the sidewalk and drove away in a beater car. The packed ashtray spewed a stream of powder down onto the carpets. The seats were buried under months of greasy fast food wrappers and the wobbly steering wheel was held together with a cross-hatch of duct tape. I turned onto the Columbia University campus.

Doubled over in the throes of another coughing fit, I lurched into the science building. Running late, I bypassed my office and went directly into the Biology Lab. The raucous roar of forty-five unsupervised students fell to silence as they scurried back to their high seats at long black tables laden with microscopes and glass beakers in assorted sizes. I launched into a lecture on Mendel's experiments on the sexual reproduction of the sweet pea.

As the discourse wound down, I removed a container from a small refrigerator. Wooden tongs in hand, I strolled out among the students, carefully placing plump peas in front of each person. "Commence dissection," I announced in a phlegm-strangled voice. In unison, students lifted scalpels and applied blades to peas. Frozen solid, the orbs immediately shot off the counters shattering vials and beakers.

"Class dismissed," I groaned.

Out in the hallway, I overheard a male student say to his partner, "Bro, how *low* did you set that 'fridge?"

I was called into the Dean of Science's office. Balding with thick grey mutton-chop sideburns and wearing low-slung reading glasses, Richard Rathbone originally from Oxford, England, listened with an air of paternal concern. I smoked while a welt from a projectile pea grew on my forehead.

"I can't take it anymore. As much as I admire Mendel, he may have led me down the wrong path. I don't know if I want to be a scientist knowing more and more about less and less…a specialist in minutia…" I was wracked by another rib-cracking cough.

"I'm quite shocked to say the least," Rathbone responded. "You are so close to finishing your Ph.D. and *peas*...everything about them has been your consuming passion for years!"

I then saw Susie's face in tears and again heard her blow me off on the phone. *"I need to study something with a heartbeat and..."* head down, I paused for a long moment. *"Emotions."*

Dean Rathbone smiled, stood up, and plucked a folder from atop a pile of papers. He walked around his desk and dropped the file into my lap. "Have just the thing. Just received this research grant…fully funded…to conduct a field study of *Orcinius Orca*."

***

I shook the memories off, threw on a coat I found in the hall closet, and walked down the long flight of stairs to the street. Out on the sidewalk I cringed as a wailing siren pierced the air. Cars whizzed by. I looked up, but couldn't find the sun or anything that resembled a blue sky. I put my head down and walked, moving slightly straighter now over the concrete. I covered the six blocks to Rathbone's brownstone and knocked on the door.

The Dean of Science appeared, looking a bit grayer and more wrinkled now. He pumped my hand, pulled me into the hallway then closed the door behind us. "Welcome home, Mr. Bachelor," Rathbone exclaimed, looking me up and down. "I must say, you've certainly changed. You've turned into bloody Tarzan!"

I shrugged and spoke slowly. "Juss a bit hard talking again after so long in the bush. And I'm not sure I know what to do about this Bachelor business."

Rathbone scoffed, "What's not to like? You're about to live every man's fantasy. Your picture is everywhere. You're six stories tall in Times Square!" He grabbed my shoulders with both hands. "God, you've turned into a handsome devil. The rigors of Alaska did you good."

I grimaced.

"What's wrong?" he asked.

"Everything feels so weird and rushed. I already miss my simple life in Alaska and I've only been back a day," I told him.

"We really should have had you come back to a halfway house or a small town like Montauk or Mendocino to ease the transition. Shock to the system. Experienced it myself after a year in the Amazon," Rathbone commented.

We talked for a few minutes about Columbia University and I caught up on the news from the science department. "Ralph took good care of my apartment. He said there are some packages for me?" I asked.

Rathbone looked me directly in the eyes. "I took a few liberties in your absence, but only to help the cause."

"What cause?"

"Come in and see," he said.

Ralph jumped up from a desk and shook my hand enthusiastically and introduced me to two other science department teaching assistants, Steve and Kwame. I felt very uncomfortable. They gazed at me in frank admiration, as if I were a god. They led me into the den now loaded and humming with the latest state-of-the-art computers, scanners, and multi-line speaker phones with all the hold buttons blinking. Tall piles of mail covered every flat surface and poured down across the floor. The scent of perfume was in the air.

The walls were papered solid with photos of women. Curvy women. Petite women. Women in revealing bikinis and buttoned-up business suits. Police and firewomen. Actresses' head shots. Women in hard hats high up on steel girders, and astride horses, camels, and elephants. Women standing proudly in puffy parkas atop snowy mountains; women in negligees reclining coyly on beds, carpets, car, and truck hoods; women clad only in garters stuffed with cash, swinging on poles.

"What's all this?" I asked, awestruck.

"Mission Control," Ralph replied.

"Since I couldn't reach you in the field," Rathbone said, "I took the liberty of setting up shop here. *Cosmopolitan* needed an address to print with your picture so readers could contact you."

Steve handed me a magazine open to the centerfold. It was the same photo from Times Square and for my Alaska book's dust jacket. I cringed at the sight of myself. Even though I was wearing a big parka, I felt totally exposed.

"And this way with everything here," Rathbone continued, "when you have women over for dates at your place they won't see any signs of the *competition.*"

Rathbone plucked a letter from a pile and read: "*Dear Michael, this is not the first time I have written to someone I don't know. The last time was to announce to a man that I was in love. The man was Elvis and I was only six. And here I am, at it again. And why you? Well, it's your desire for adventure, as well as the fact that you actually followed through with that desire that I find attractive...*"

The three assistants whooped and hollered. Like a fish out of water my mouth opened and closed without a sound coming out. With the phones ringing and machines humming the assistants turned back to their positions. Kwame, originally from Ghana, West Africa, and hoping to return home with an Environmental Studies degree, answered the phones. Ralph, a Zoology major from Brooklyn wearing a *Save the Males* button, monitored the e-mails.

Steve, the only married man and an assistant professor in Physics, answered the door and returned with his arms full of mail, flowers, and gift boxes. While I stood dumbstruck to one side, they sorted through the packages and letters. The letters were written on everything from panties to birch bark and in every hue of ink. Quite a few were covered with lipstick kisses.

"You're a *Swak Daddy*!" Steve exclaimed.

"You mean *Mack Daddy*," Kwame corrected.

"No, man, *S.W.A.K.*—Sealed-With-A-Kiss," Steve beamed, holding up a luscious imprint of ruby red lips.

"You'll never be able to commit to one," Ralph sighed, flipping through the day's letters and photos. "Always wondering what tomorrow's mail will bring..."

"Yeah," Kwame added, "bed 'em, don't wed 'em."

They took turns reading letters aloud. One came from a mother who wrote recommending her daughter…*and if she doesn't work out—call ME!* A CEO wanted to rendezvous in Tahiti with all expenses paid. A Hollywood film producer and former Rose Bowl Parade Queen started out, "I've never done anything like this before..."

"OK," Ralph interrupted, "where's the kicker?"

"Tha wha…?" I asked, still having difficulty speaking.

"Every woman who starts out a letter like that," Steve said, "and believe me there are lots, always slips in something risqué at the end. Kwame, find it?"

"Yeah," Kwame said, "check this: '*PS: If you come see me I promise to blow your socks off!!*'"

"Socks or rocks?" Ralph snorted.

They all laughed, except me.

Ralph entered the particulars from the day's mail into the computer. He showed me how I could find individual women I might be interested in by entering in the Search field specific hair color or body type.

"The mail contains more than letters..." Steve paused to extract an article of clothing from a large padded envelope. He slung a huge bra across the table. It had a note pinned to it: *This is just the package. If you want the contents call (201) 364-7186! Love, Desiree.* Grasping one end of the bra, Steve handed the other end to Kwame. They walked the bra into Rathbone's kitchen followed by the others.

Steve plucked two grapefruits out of a bowl and dropped them into the cups of the brassiere. They disappeared.

"Another thing," Ralph remarked, "most of these girls' mothers must have really been into romance novels. We've been seeing very few *Marys*, *Janes*, or *Susans*. The common *Cosmo* girls' names are Samantha, Cassandra, Mandy, or…"

"Desiree!" Steve chortled, while sliding two eggplants into the bra, finally filling the cups. We all stared in awe.

Returning to the den, Kwame said, "Check these phone messages. The first one called collect."

He punched a button. "Hi, Michael, this is Deloris. I've been a prisoner since 1991, get out in a few weeks and need a boyfriend bad! There are five hundred women here in The Broward Correctional Institution in Florida. Someone must have bribed a guard to run off your picture on the copy machine 'cause when I was walkin' out to the exercise yard today, I saw you up on nearly every woman's wall. It gets so hot and humid that it rains inside this friggin' place. You being in snow and up in Alaska and all, you're more than just a hunk a' man, you're the very symbol of freedom to us." *Beep.*

"Next one," Kwame continued, "came through the international operator."

"Dis be Dolly from de Gran Caimon, mon. Doncha be foolin' wit nun a' dos stick bitches, dos bony-ass white gals! Come to dee islands and Dolly show you what reel lovin' is like!"

I shook my head in disbelief.

Ralph moved to the computer and called for attention. He tapped keys and read off statistics, "So far, 4,594 letters, packages, and phone calls. On the internet alone where *Cosmo* has you on their website you're getting five hundred hits a day."

"What part of the country has written the most?" Steve inquired.

Ralph rapped a few keys. "The South, three to one."

Steve riffled through a pile of mail to locate a letter. "Let's call Robbi from Atlanta. She might give us an idea why that is."

I fearfully shook my head and stepped back in retreat.

"Since you're having trouble talking, I'll just pretend I'm you," Steve said.

I looked at Rathbone, who smiled and shrugged.

Steve punched in Robbi's number on the speaker phone. She answered. Pretending he was me, he informed her of the finding and asked, "Why the American South?"

"Dahlin', that's easy. We've all grown up on *Gone with the Wind* and we're lookin' for Rhett. We want a man who's a tad bit reckless and very, very romantic. But today Rhett Butler is on the Endangered Species List. We're more likely to meet

Bigfoot. Men use romance to hook you, but after a while that well runs *drab!*"

Steve thanked her for her opinion and said goodbye, hanging up the phone. Silence hung heavily in the room.

"*Gone with the Wind* and back with the breeze," Ralph said.

Seeing that I was both overwhelmed and exhausted, Rathbone said, "Come on, I'll walk you home."

As we walked along in the cold evening, Rathbone inquired, "How do you feel about all this?"

"Well, I'm pissed. Not at you and the guys. What you've done is amazing. Thank you. It's just that I never had a choice in the matter and with my first book I want to be taken seriously as a scientist. As a Cosmo *Bachelor,* I'll be the laughing stock of academia."

"Exactly my first reaction when I heard about it from Liz. But, you know, after giving it some thought and sifting through some of the actual data my deeper hunch is holding true."

"Which is?" I asked.

"It's the very opposite of frivolous; this opportunity that has presented itself. Think about it. When in ten lifetimes, if ever, does a man receive a chance like this?"

"What? To notch my bedpost to the nth degree?"

"No, to study women, the *female animal,* as you did wildlife."

I stopped walking. "You're serious?"

"Yes! You've more than proven that you're a qualified researcher and done so in the most challenging of conditions. Your findings are brilliant. Your Killer Whale book is a landmark work; a lodestar full of original discoveries."

"But those were whales—dolphins, actually—these are *women.*" We walked on but Rathbone couldn't let it go.

"Yes, and now you are perfectly prepared. You've just come away from studying one of the most intelligent, complex, and dangerous creatures on earth. Why not study women and their behavior: mating habits and such, as you did the dolphins?"

"Have you gone off the deep end?" I asked.

"No. Do it all analytically. Leave your emotions out of it or you'll lose your controls. And with this incredibly broad database, no pun intended, you just may come out of this with answers substantiated by hard facts. Think of it, with your findings you could alleviate the suffering of half of mankind!"

I felt both terrified and intrigued. "How so?"

"You are like a living laboratory," Rathbone continued. "Many people seeking a partner are faced with the perplexity of choice. But in your case the number of choices is off the charts. It will be most interesting to see how you navigate through this rich entanglement of biodiversity," Rathbone paused, and his voice took on a more paternal tone. "And more importantly, I'm curious to see what happens to you personally. Who knows? You might meet someone you feel serious about."

"Even if I did decide to do it, how would I fund this study? Dolphins are cheap; women are expensive as I recall. And I know nothing about women. Had one girlfriend my whole life and she blew me off big time."

Undaunted, Rathbone's face erupted into a *Cheshire Cat* grin. "We struck while the proverbial *iron was hot.* With advance reviews of the Alaska book so glowing, your publisher was an easy sell. Liz landed you an advance for this new book based on a synopsis she and I drew up." He plucked a check from his jacket pocket and rapped it with the back of his hand. "This ought to arm you with a few bouquets of flowers."

Standing at the entrance of my apartment building, I examined the check. I pursed my lips and gave a low whistle.

Rathbone gandy-danced away then stopped and turned around. "And having been away a long time you now possess the asset hardest for a scientist to acquire."

"Which is?"

"A fresh perspective," he replied.

***

I sat on the couch staring straight ahead. I couldn't believe how fast my life had flipped. I exhaled a long sigh. *Glad*

*Rathbone and the guys have everything over there so I can have my own space and peace. Maybe the TAs should date the girls. They're way more into it than I am.*

I absentmindedly clicked on the TV. The movie *Jaws* was on. In a lull between attacks from the great white shark, the three men were gathered inside the battered boat comparing scars from past wildlife encounters. I leaned forward intently waiting for my favorite scene in the film when the great actor Robert Shaw as Captain Quint describes being aboard the USS Indianapolis during World War II when it was torpedoed and sunk by a Japanese sub: *...eleven hundred men went into the water...three hundred and sixteen come out… the sharks took the rest...*

After the scene I snapped off the TV and went to bed, improvising with a squint my favorite line from Captain Quint, "A shark's got doll's eyes. Ya don't think it's alive until it bites ya."

I awoke the next morning feeling refreshed. Looking around the bedroom, I thought back to the Victoria's Secret catalog model pinned, in sheer desperation, up on the wall of my Alaskan cabin. I thought of all the pictures of women, many just as beautiful, over in Mission Control, who now wanted to meet me.

My thoughts flashed to what Lucy the Native Elder had said when I left: *Where you are going is far more dangerous...* However, after surviving Alaska, danger now intrigued me. And women, I sensed, were very much like Alaska: a combination of beauty and danger.

Surrounded now by the comforts I'd left behind and adjusting again to civilization, I felt dulled. I needed a new challenge to keep and hone my edge. But deep down I'd always been afraid of women. *We fear what we don't know.* I then remembered what Dean Rathbone had once taught me about going into the unknown: *Replace fear with knowledge.*

# 3

# Behind Enemy Lines

Monday evening, after Rathbone and the teaching assistants were finished with their classes, we huddled together at Mission Control conducting a *Cosmo* clinic. Ralph had raided the magazine rack at his dentist's office and now dropped a copy of *Cosmopolitan* in front of each man. Like spies behind enemy lines, we closely scrutinized the magazines as if trying to decipher secret codes.

"What headlines," Ralph said, tapping the front cover. "*TAKE YOUR CLIMAX TO THE MAX: Discover Your Amazing Moan Zone!*"

We looked up at each other in disbelief.

He continued reading: "*GIVE HIM A WILD WAKE-UP CALL: Set the buzzer for Sex o'clock!* and, *HIS BUTT: What the Size, Shape, and Pinchability of Those Sweet Cheeks Reveal About His True Self.*"

We whooped and hollered.

"*Moan Zone*. I'm down with that," Kwame said.

"Next time a woman asks me what time it is," Ralph chortled, "I'm gonna say Sex o'clock!"

"Hmm," Steve murmured, studying his issue. "There's a section in here that looks to be a regular feature called *MAN MANUAL*..."

"Hey Ralph," Kwame said. "Check this: *ARE MEN BECOMING OBSOLETE? Take-Charge Chicks Are Surpassing Guys in Many Areas.*"

Ralph raised the middle finger on one hand and lifted up the omnipresent *SAVE THE MALES* button on his shirt with his other hand.

Steve looked at me. "Hey dude, we're way more into all this than you are. What's up?"

I shrugged. "Like the drug dealer said to Scarface, 'Don't get high on your own supply.' "

"Scarface also said," Ralph grabbed his crotch, " 'Say hello to my little friend!' "

Everyone except Ralph burst out laughing. "Trying to tell us something?" Kwame asked.

"I meant the machine gun," Ralph smirked.

"Bro, promise us one thing," Kwame said, turning toward me.

"What's that?"

"Promise you'll never get married. Look at all this!" Kwame waved his arms around the room. "You can tag a different girl every night for ten lifetimes."

"Marriage is a three-ring circus," Ralph said. "Engagement ring. Wedding ring. Suffering."

"Nah," Steve, the married man, added. "You guys have it all wrong. My wife and I were happy for twenty years—and then we met."

We all laughed.

"Good one, Stevo," Ralph said.

"True?" I inquired.

"Naw, it's a great life with the right wife. Marriage has a huge upside."

"Then what are you doing here?" I said.

"Not sure and want to find out," Steve shrugged, turning back to his magazine. "What I'm getting from *MAN MANUAL* is that most of this is a dichotomy. Even though women no longer need us like maybe our mothers needed our fathers financially, they are taught in article after article specifically how to get us to commit—get that ring and us around their little fingers. Never realized it was such a widespread, covert operation."

Ralph hammered a fist down on the table. "To commit to one woman slams the door on the single most powerful force that drives us. By our very nature, men are NOT monogamous. It's built-in, hard-wired that monogamy is monotony."

"Just not realistic—the *till death do you part* bit," Kwame said. "Getting married means that's the last and final girl I'm going to have sex with for fifty years? No way! And it's not fair. We get the short end of the deal. Stray once and you lose your house and half your income? Count me out."

"Hell," Ralph said, "I don't even want to see anyone that many days in a row. There are very few women I'd want to spend my life with, but thousands of them I want to spend one night with."

"Ralph's right," Kwame said matter-of-factly. "It's just not in our nature to be faithful. Women produce one egg a month. Men make two hundred million sperm a day. You do the math."

I turned to Rathbone. "What do you make of all this?"

"As the old Bard said, 'no one will ever win the battle of the sexes. There's too much fraternizing with the enemy.'"

***

The next day it was one of those autumnal New York days where the city seemed to shine and sparkle. The north wind freshened and invigorated the air and the sun glowed like butterscotch. I bought a *New York Times* newspaper at a sidewalk kiosk and walked into my favorite neighborhood diner for lunch. Inside the restaurant everything was as though I had never left. There was the same great aroma of onions and cooked red meat and as usual the place was packed with people. I walked over the cracked and pitted linoleum to the only unoccupied table back by the swinging kitchen doors.

Scanning the many entrees on the faded menu, I thought of how I had eaten in singular cycles in Alaska. Catch a big salmon and feast on it all week. Pull up the crab trap in the back bay and munch and crunch day and night until my fingers ached from cracking shells. Dig clams from the beach at low tide and go on a sweet, extended, mollusk feast. All were now thrown together before me in a delicious seafood soup. As I ate, I savored each collective sip and bite.

Scanning the newspaper I was thinking, *new names; same old crimes.* Glancing over the top of the paper, I saw that instead of eating many people were staring at a table in the far corner. Food was being ignored. Cell phones were lifted and voices were spattered with excitement. Women got up from their seats and stepped toward the table, wide-eyed and smiling. I recognized the object of their affections. *That famous actor, Chad or Brad....*

The actor jumped up, dropped money on the table, and head down, strode quickly toward the door to the kitchen. He stopped alongside my table. "Hey, *Cosmo* guy! Saw you in Times Square, man. FOREVER WILD!" he said, with his hand squaring the words in the air. He glanced over his shoulder. More women poured into the diner.

"The female lions do the hunting," the actor said. "Saw it on some animal show." He pushed through the back door and escaped into the cover of the urban jungle.

With the subjects clearly defined, certainly intriguing, and the danger level ramped up high enough, I was now more receptive to both dating and studying the *Cosmo* girls. One evening in my new favorite place, the shower, I felt my emotions suddenly switch from doubt to certitude.

I threw on some new clothes I'd bought and charged out the door, game face on, bounding over to Mission Control with a song running through my mind: *"Get your motor runnin'/Head out on the highway/ Lookin' for adventure/And whatever comes our way/Yeah, Darlin' go make it happen/Take the world in a love embrace.... I like smoke and lightning.* I winked at a woman passing me on the sidewalk. *Heavy metal thundah.* I blew a kiss to a pierced and tattooed hottie across the street. *Racin' with the wiiiiind/And the feelin' that I'm under/Like a true nature's child/We were born, born to be wild/We can climb so high/I never wanna diiiie/* I jumped Rathbone's steps three-at-a-time and exploded through the door. *Born to be Wild!/Born to be Wiiild!!*

I stood there, legs apart, chest heaving. Rathbone and the TAs came out of Mission Control. I lifted my hands up and flipped my fingers back, "Bring it on."

They hollered and we high-fived all around. "Let the Grand Game begin," Rathbone announced.

"That's what I'm talking about!" Kwame said.

"Have we got a first date for you," Ralph added.

"Bro, you got *Mad* game comin'…" Kwame dropped a letter and pictures on a table. "Shareen Burri. She's a body-double in Hollywood. Bills herself as *The Best Butt in the Business* and she's all that. Baby Got *Baack!*"

We gathered around the pictures.

"Well…?" Kwame asked.

"Sweet," I said, trying to appear nonchalant while my heart was jack-hammering with excitement and fear.

"Take a seat, Michael," Rathbone said, pulling out a chair. "Since you've been gone a long time there are a few things you should know before this study gets underway."

They reminded me that AIDS was still around and that various STDs were now widespread and nasty.

"And don't forget what happened a long time ago," Ralph said.

"What's that?" I said.

"Lorena Bobbitt…slicing off husband John's penis with a knife," Ralph continued, "I know it was a million years ago but as the saying goes, 'He who does not know history is fated to repeat it.'"

"Another thing," Steve said.

"Not sure I want to hear it," I mumbled, grimacing after the Bobbitt reminder.

"Big movement while you were gone and still going on for men to be feminized," Steve said. "Think that music show host… all twirly and girly."

"Who?" I asked.

"Yeah, don't go there, bro," Kwame added.

Steve continued. "Women try to change you to be like them, but once you're a girly man they don't want you anymore.

The good girls want the bad boys or else they get bored. Keep it wild."

"Yeah, and don't ever cry," Ralph said. "Well, maybe shed a few if you're forced to endure some sensitive chick-flick, but only if there's *payoff* at the end."

I stood up, nodding my head. "A lot to process. Thanks, guys."

"Report back here right after Shareen," Steve said. "That's an order."

Rathbone walked me to the door. "Above all be careful out there."

I turned around slowly. "That Bobbit guy…they really did find his penis and they really sewed it back on, right?"

"Yep," Ralph said. "Cops found his dick in the weeds alongside a 7-11 in Manassas, Virginia. Imagine the police radio dispatcher putting out that call." Ralph hunched forward in front of the computer, talking into an imaginary microphone. "Now hear this. All-points bulletin. Be on the lookout for a missing penis. The victim is approximately one to nine inches tall, more likely on the short side with major shrinkage and profuse bleeding. Can't get far on his own and not known whether the vic is wearing a hood or bare-headed. If found, please return missing trouser trout—STAT—to rightful owner. Search for penis only. Testicles are intact. Repeat—wife left testicles intact."

We laughed and winced at the same time.

"Used to be 'Vagina dentate,' " Steve said. "A man was afraid to have sex with a woman because there might be teeth down there."

"Ah, yes," Rathbone chortled. "A man enters triumphant and leaves diminished."

"Now there are knives," Steve said.

"And guns," Kwame added. "In the Hood last week, girl blows her player boyfriend away. One shot between the eyes with a Glock Nine."

"And cars," Steve said. "Woman caught her man with another woman and ran him over in the hotel parking lot and kept backing over him, back and forth, until he was a bloody, pulpy mess."

"Michael," Ralph said, looking up from the computer.

"Yeah," I gulped, now afraid to go out the door.

"Lock and load," Ralph said resolutely.

"Mike," Steve said.

"What?"

"...catch and release my friend... catch and release."

Facing my first date in over five years I reverted back to high school when I used to stare at the phone in a nervous, cold sweat before summoning the courage to call a girl and ask her out. Now with the level of women elevated considerably my palms were wet. Even though I knew I was now accepted, wanted even, old habits die hard. Finally, I grabbed the phone and quickly punched in Shareen Burri's cell phone number in Los Angeles.

She answered as if expecting me. "Hi, babe. I'm on the set. Can't talk long."

"I have to be out in California—San Francisco, for a book signing on Friday. Any way that maybe we could get together?"

"Sure. We wrap today and I'm free Friday. I'll jump on the shuttle from L.A. I have bonus miles to burn."

"Really? Um...well...e-mail me your flight and I'll pick you up."

"*Kuhl,* cutie. We'll have fun!"

I gave her my e-mail address and hung up the phone.

Early Friday morning, I flew across the country to San Francisco. Following the instructions Liz sent, I rented a car and drove to the bookstore to do the signing. On the expressway I crept along in the slow lane with a white-knuckled grip on the steering wheel. I was so used to bobbing along at kayak-pace on the ocean that the speed limit of seventy felt rocket-fast.

When I walked through the back door of the bookstore, the owner swooped down on me. "Thank God you're here! They're lined up out the door and we're calling around to other stores for more books. KPIX, Channel Five, is already out there setting up their lights. Can I get you anything—coffee, tea, water?"

"Water is fine."

The owner returned with a bottle of water. "You're doing something very few authors can do," she said, leading me to the book signing table at the front of the store.

"What's that?"

"Bringing an entirely new demographic into the store."

I looked out the large front window and my jaw dropped. On the sidewalk was a line of young women. I went to the window and looked down the side of the store. The line extended as far as I could see.

I settled in and the owner signaled a staff member who opened the front door. The crowd surged in.

"Who can I sign to?" I asked the first woman in line.

I signed my Alaska book and *Cosmopolitan* magazines and jumped up for pictures. Each time the woman moved in close alongside me. The feel of a female pressed against my side with her slender arm around me, her hand resting on my hip, and her perfume or fresh natural scent rising like sweet ambrosia around me, made my head spin and heart flip. I placed my hand carefully on each woman's waist and held on and so did they, squeezing in even tighter as we smiled together for the camera.

I put my head down and signed and signed, trying to focus on the book, feeling amazed and so grateful that my solitary adventures in Alaska were now going out into a receptive world.

Feeling the table shake, I looked up and saw a pair of gigantic breasts looming directly in front of me. Barely held in check inside a skimpy halter top, the breasts stopped inches from my eyes as the woman leaned forward with her hands planted out to the sides.

"I'm not much of a reader. Would you sign here instead?" she said, swiveling her shoulders.

The paired orbs bobbed with hefty pulchritude and seemed to expand even larger through the air, filling a man who for so long was far removed from female bounty. A line from a

Theodore Roethke poem sprang to mind: "She moved in circles and those circles moved."

"I call them the *Girls*," she said.

My hand slid higher up the barrel of the Mont Blanc pen and I lifted it like a cautious mountain climber with ice spike in hand. On a plateau safely above the twin summits, I scrawled: *To the most beautiful Girls in the world! M.M.*

"Who can I sign to?" I blurted quickly to the next woman. The heat-flush slowly faded from my face as I went on a rapid run of signing books.

Another woman reached forward and plucked away my pen. She took up my left hand, opened my palm and scrawled her phone number on it. As she closed my fingers with hers time stood still, silence reigned, and my heart boomed. She held me in her curled hand and stared invitingly into my eyes. As if in slow motion she opened her mouth and bright white teeth bit down on the center of her pink, pillow-plump bottom lip.

"Who can.... How can.... OH, GOD," I said, dropping my head.

The line broke apart and reformed behind the table. Cheerleaders from the nearby University of California wanted a picture. Fresh from practice, they were still in their uniforms.

"Where do you want me?" I innocently asked.

"In the middle," the captain commanded. I stepped forward and was engulfed in a cross-hatch of slender arms and hands. Again, I inhaled that alluring feminine scent and firm, bare thighs pressed forth from me a deep sigh and the thought: *When that grizzly bear attacked in Alaska maybe I did die, and this is Heaven?*

Finally, the end was near. After signing for the last woman, I stood up and was immediately blinded by lights as a reporter for KPIX-TV stuck a microphone in my face.

"So, how does it feel to be the Hunk of the Month?"

"Overwhelming and a bit scary."

"Oh, come on," she teased. "Those women all *loved* you!"

"That's the problem."

"How so?"

"It's like going from famine to feast and I don't even know how to use a fork."

As if floating in a dream, I made my way out the back door of the bookstore with the owner happily blowing me a kiss as I departed.

# 4

# The Weaker Sex

**Shareen Burri**
**Species Name:** *Babi Gotbooti*
**Habitat & Range:** Neighborhood Multiplex Theaters.
**Identifying Characteristics:** Gluteus to the Maximus.
**Best Known For:** Stopping traffic.

*Now—Shareen.* Heart pounding I sped off to the airport and left the car in short-term parking ,walked to the gate and waited. Drying my sweating hands on my pants the ink from the phone number on my palm smeared across my left front thigh. *Shit!* There was no time to run to the Men's room.

The plane's walkway door opened and Shareen Burri was the second person off. She moved toward me in stiletto heels, jeans so tight they looked painted-on and a tiny, hot-pink baby-tee. Platinum blonde hair threw off brilliant light and up close her turquoise eyes sparkled. The only flaw to actress perfection was a strong blade of a nose.

"Yum," she said, looking me up and down.

"Gorgeous," I told her.

As we walked away from the gate, she said, "What's that on your pants?"

"Oh, ink."

"Pen break?"

"No, a phone number."

"What?"

I explained.

"That's so sweet that I made you sweat!"

She told me that she'd checked a bag so we went down the escalator to the baggage carousel. We didn't wait long before she pointed to the largest suitcase I had ever seen in my life. It was immense, mammoth, the *Peterbilt* of suitcases, it should have had a set of tires and an air-horn attached.

I bent my knees, power lifting it off the platform. "Isn't this a bit much for an overnighter?" I inquired.

She flashed a wicked grin. "I brought a few surprises."

In the car on the freeway heading back to San Francisco, we chatted about the movie business. I asked, "What film were you working on when I called?"

"An action thriller. Do you know what Sharon Stone said to me first day on the set?"

"What?"

"I finally get my Dream Butt!"

"You mean the actress picks?"

"Yes."

"How?"

"Agent sends over my shots."

"Pictures of just your butt?"

"Yep. I send what they want to show—tight shots of my ass."

"Don't you find that at all, well, demeaning?"

Shareen smirked. "Last year, I had 500,000 reasons not to."

I lifted an eyebrow. "You made that much…good for you."

We found The White Swan Inn in downtown San Francisco, but there was no place to park. Finally, at the bottom of a steep hill I spotted a small space and after four tries I managed to cram the car in.

"Sorry. I haven't driven or parallel parked in a while. Hope you don't mind the walk," I said and grimaced remembering her monster suitcase.

"No, the exercise will do me good," she replied.

We started up the long hill. Struggling with the bag, I fell behind Shareen. A man walking downhill passed her, his head doing a near *Exorcist* spin. Atop the hill a cable car full of people headed down the middle of the street. All the men's heads swiveled as one. A man in a suit, gripping a briefcase in one hand and a brass pole in the other, leaned out so far to follow Shareen's mesmerizing sashay that he lost his grip and tumbled out onto the street. Higher up the hill, drivers of two cars careened their necks and crashed head-on into each other. Their cars slid slowly down the hill crumpled together.

To halt further mayhem, I charged up the hill and grabbed Shareen by the arm, stopping her. "Do you see the wake behind you?"

She slapped the side of her hip. "It's a weapon of *ass* destruction. Wanna know my secret?"

"What?"

"I stole it from Marilyn Monroe. She shaved an eighth-of-an-inch off the bottom of her right heel. Puts the wiggle in the walk," she giggled and continued up the hill spinning more heads and steering wheels each cantilevered step of the way.

We checked into The White Swan. The hefty, older woman behind the desk looked Shareen up and down disapprovingly while I filled out the form.

"There are tea and crumpets and a selection of sherries downstairs in front of the fireplace for happy hour," the innkeeper said. She stared at the giant suitcase then glanced at the tattered backpack slung over my shoulders. "I'll have the, ahem, bags sent up to your room. You are staying just one night, right?"

In a drawing room at the bottom of the stairs congregated around a crackling fire was a large group of Stanford University alumni in town for the big football game against the University of California. All were middle-aged and upper-class doctors and lawyers dressed in Stanford's Cardinal Red.

When Shareen reached the bottom step the room fell silent. She walked slowly toward the fireplace. The women flung eye-darts at her. The men all tilted in her direction.

Shareen swung around with her backside to the flames. Always the actress, she flipped her platinum blonde hair over her shoulder, parked an elbow on the mantel piece, licked her lips, and whispered, "Where can a girl get a drink around here?" The men rushed her with glasses of sherry sloshing onto their shoes.

An elderly man in a far corner, his feet shuffling up and down, was admonished by his seething wife, "George, put your tongue back in your mouth!"

I caught Shareen's eye then slid my extended index finger under my nose pointing back up the stairs. As she sauntered toward me the crowd parted like the Red Sea. As we left, the inebriated and those men immune for whatever reasons to married fury leered longingly up the stairs.

We made our way to the room.

"Look at this place," she said, eyes gliding over the peach-colored, flocked wallpaper, overstuffed chairs, and a white wicker goose with trailing goslings on an antique oak table. "Laura Ashley to the max. My grandma would love this place. Why did you choose *this*?"

"I didn't. The bookstore owner did."

I threw myself on the frilly bed, suddenly feeling battered by the backwash of being with a bona fide sex symbol. "I can't believe how you totally blew up that room, or the street for that matter."

"You know," she said as she settled into a poufy chair, "as you just saw, women are far more competitive than men. When a woman walks into a room what's the first thing she sees?"

"The men."

"Wrong. The first thing she looks at is the other women. She scopes out the prettiest woman there so she knows who her competition is. You saw it work in reverse today. To married women, all other women are *The Enemy*, a threat of taking away their husbands." She sighed. "All my girlfriends who are married, who I used to have so much fun with now want nothing to do with me."

"That's sad."

"Yep, marriage is an institution, and I don't want to be committed."

"Hey, are you hungry? Want some dinner?" I said.

Shareen gave her wicked grin again. "Hungry, yes…but not for food. We'll do that after. Be right back." She slid her huge suitcase toward the bathroom, turned around and winked. "I like to primp before I pump."

After much thumping in the bathroom, she called: "ARE YOU READEEE?"

I didn't answer. My heart raced as I wondered, *I've heard of life in the fast lane, but we're talking flat out turbo-charged here!*

"HELLO."

"Yess," I said, cotton-mouthed as I reclined on the bed.

She walked out wearing nothing but a tool belt…a yellow-suede, multi-pouched holder filled with sex toys. She turned around and my heart jumped. It framed her perfect hips like chaps without legs.

"I used to be a carpenter before I hit it big with my butt. The belt still comes in handy." She ran through a quick inventory, holding each item up for inspection: fur-lined handcuffs, Jane's Bonds, a riding crop, can of whipped cream, ribbed condoms…

"No wearing 'em inside-out!"

…Catapult lubricant, "Warms when yah blow on it," she explained.

The Vibro-Sleeve and Fireman's Pump, "Toys for Boys."

The Triple-Ripple, "For backdoor play."

She then pulled out the heavy artillery—vibrators: Pocket Rocket, G-Spotter, and The Night Rider, "Comes with strong straps, so I can put it anywhere on you and *Yee haw*…buck away to my heart's content. The first few orgasms are just foreplay in my book."

Working her way around to the back, from low-slung pockets she pulled out a tape measure and duct tape. "Oops!

From my last real job." And then from a deep pouch on the other side, out came a small clear bubble with a magnetic needle inside.

"What's that?"

"Stud-finder," she giggled, holding it out over me. "Guess we won't be needing this."

"Sooo," she said, hooking her thumbs into the front of the tool belt and sticking out a hip, "what do you want first?"

I gulped…"A kiss?"

***

On the plane ride home, I pulled out my laptop from my backpack and wrote:

*THEOREM #1: THE WEAKER SEX*

Shareen Burri totally lived up to her billing of *The Best Butt in the Business.* If you draw the symbol for Love ♥—that is the exact shape of Shareen's butt. She has a tiny waist from which each cheek swells to curved perfection—tight, hard, yet oh so smooth melons you could bounce quarters off of, and I did.... well, actually AA batteries. Her perfect butt was covered with a field of tiny golden hairs, like spun gold, gossamer silk—slightly nappy to the touch. The hairs seemed most concentrated in a small thatch at her coccyx or tailbone. Beneath the Hollywood beauty there lurked a primordial beast!

Coincidentally, on the plane ride out here, in the scientific journal, *Nature*, I had just read that all mammals have a tail at one point in their development. In humans it is present for a period of four weeks during stages fourteen to twenty-two of embryogenesis.

Evolution has crafted the female human animal with a form so alluring that it drives men wild. If sex is dirty or bad, then why are women's bodies so sexualized—the cut out waist, flaring hips, and round breasts. There are no straight lines in nature, nor do there appear to be any on the female body. Spherical miracles!

And women are the stronger sex by far, for they possess a power that even slightly revealed reduces men to salivating slaves and gibbering idiots. *Girls rule; guys drool.* Coupling all that power and flexibility with carpenter skills, tricks of the trade from a deep tool belt, and sex becomes a shocking, erotic adventure.

So much for women not being able to have sex without falling in love. Shareen was the predator, I the prey. And I'm now praying even though we had very little to talk about that in this lifetime sex like this happens at least once, no five, oh, hell—at least one hundred times MORE!

***

Rathbone picked me up at the airport and we zoomed back to Mission Control. The TAs were eagerly awaiting a full report. I told them about the gawker falling off the cable car, the cars crashing, the reception of the stuffy Stanford guests, and the Marilyn Monroe high heel reveal. Pressed for details of what went on behind closed doors, I gave the inventory of Shareen's tool belt and left it at that.

"Tape measure?" Ralph uncomfortably inquired.

"Duct tape!" Steve stated in awe.

"As far as going further in front of this Grand Inquisition and thus incriminating myself unfairly, I have no choice, but…" I raised my right hand, "to plead the Fifth." I made a zipper motion across my lips.

"Well," Ralph smiled, "have we got a next date for you."

"You won't believe who wrote in!" Steve beamed.

"Who?"

"MANDY TYLER!!!" they chorused.

"Who's she?"

"Dude! Where you been, living on an island? Well, DUH. She…" Ralph said, dropping her picture and letter in front of me, "…is one of the hottest porn stars on the planet!"

I picked up her photograph, looking through a mash of fingerprints on the revealing, glossy shot. "Never seen her before."

"Damn, you got to catch up, bro," Kwame said.

I walked over to a big box filled with mail. "What's this?"

"Instant rejects," Ralph said, tilting a thumb down.

I picked up the box. "Just going to give it a look."

# 5

# Doctor Devi

**<u>Devi Rangashar</u>**
**Species Name:** *Studius Medicus Indius*
**Habitat & Range:** Sterile wards.
**Identifying Characteristics:** Tired, ruffled feathers.
**Best Known For:** A Beautiful Mind.

With a strong cup of coffee in hand the next morning, I started in on the box of rejected mail. I pulled a letter out randomly and read:

*Dear Michael,*

*I really don't know why I'm bothering to write to you. You won't write or call with all the women after you and I don't have the time, anyway. I'm in my sixth year of medical school and doing my residency at Mt. Sinai. I just read your book and admire you for your work with whales. If I wasn't going to be a doctor, I would have gone into Marine Biology. I dream constantly of swimming with dolphins…that is when I have time to sleep.*

*Take care,*
*Devi Rangashar*

There was no return address, but beneath her name I saw a phone number, barely discernible. *She already has the doctor's scrawl.* I dialed two different wrong numbers before I got it right. Devi identified herself on voice mail. I left a message, saying how impressed I was by her letter and asked her to please call me back.

I went off to the gym, vowing to keep in Alaska shape. Afterwards, I stopped at the neighborhood diner for a salad. I walked home feeling much better about life and myself. Rather than just following the testosterone-driven whims of the TAs, I now felt in better control of the dates.

The phone rang in the middle of the night. I bolted out of bed smashing my toes against the end bed post and hopped, aching foot in hand, to the phone.

"Michael?"

"Yes."

"I'm sorry, I was expecting your machine. This is Devi; it's the only time I can call." She spoke with a slight British accent.

"It's OK."

"What's wrong? You sound in pain."

"Just smashed my toes."

"Oh, I shouldn't have called. Never mind!"

"No, wait. Do you want to get together?"

"Really?"

"Yes. When are you free?"

"Now—this time, for lunch."

I picked up the clock. "Two a.m.?"

"Yes. I'm a resident at Mt. Sinai Hospital. It's really the only time I have free."

"OK. When and where?"

"Here—at the hospital. Tomorrow night?"

"Great."

"You sure?"

"Yes."

"I'll x-ray your toes..."

I entered Mt. Sinai Hospital and found Devi waiting at the security desk in the lobby. She was short with black cropped hair, thick glasses and purple circles under her eyes. The guard asked to inspect my backpack.

"Well, there goes the surprise," I said.

"Look at all this great food!" she said, her British accent stronger in person.

"From Zabar's—thought we'd have a picnic."

"I go there sometimes just to walk around and make a meal of all the samples," Devi said. "Then I feel so guilty, I buy a token tin of exotic olives or something that ends up costing me way more than if I'd just bought a sandwich to begin with."

I laughed. "I used to do the same thing when I was studying for my doctorate."

"So, we're both doctors."

"Me, sort of, you—definitely. Where should we go to eat?"

"I know, this way." She led me down the hall toward the elevator. "How are your toes?" she asked.

"Fine, just jammed them on the bed post."

"I felt so bad calling you so late, but this really is the only time I have." Inside the elevator she blew her nose like a trumpet. "Horrible health habits—no sleep, junk food, always sick while learning to be a doctor."

The elevator door opened and she approached a door on the right. She pulled out a key card and swiped it alongside the door, unlocking the lab. She flicked on the lights. I reached out and flicked them off.

"What are you doing!" she exclaimed.

I pulled two round candles out of my pack. "*Voilà!*"

"Oh, a romantic."

I lit the squat candles and spread the food out on a clear counter. My eyes darted around the lab. I took a deep breath and puffed out my chest, "I love the smell of formaldehyde in the morning. It smells like...."

"VICTORY!" we both shouted.

"*Apocalypse Now*—I loved that movie," she said.

Then as if suddenly retreating from having unfamiliar fun a shadow passed over Devi's face and she said sternly, "So, why me? Is this some sort of mercy mission?"

"Whoa," I exhaled.

"Sorry. It's just with all those women to pick from...."

"Can I ask you something?"

She stared hard at me for a moment, then nodded.

"Why bother to write if you didn't think I would see you?"

"My mother bought me the subscription to *Cosmo.* She's always after me to be more feminine or…'You'll never catch a husband!' Guess she's right, but I'm just not into that whole girly thing. Too much time, effort, and money—none of which I have right now."

"That's why I wanted to see you."

"Why? Because I'm ugly, broke, and exhausted?"

"No, because you're dedicated to a noble cause and have an I.Q. bigger than your shoe size, which make you attractive."

"Oh."

"Devi, I had a taste of what you're going through when I got my doctorate. A beautiful mind is just as attractive to me as a sexy body."

"Really?"

"Yes."

We paused to bite into our sandwiches. "What type of doctor are you studying to be?" I asked.

"OB/GYN. I love the idea of bringing children into the world. Do you want kids?"

"I go back and forth. The number one reason why the environment is so damaged, in such trouble, is there are too many people on Earth. And the population explosion shows no signs of slowing down. It's like a virulent cancer attacking the land. However, I love kids."

"I see your point about overpopulation. Especially every time I go back to India."

"Ah, what Socrates said we all should be: a citizen of the world, with a global perspective."

She nodded in agreement. "Especially in this day and age."

"So ridiculous, all the rampant nationalism and racism. I think the space program during the sixties was all worth it for just one picture. Do you know that shot the astronauts took of *Earth Rising* where the planet looked like a gleaming blue marble suspended in space?"

"Yes. I had the poster on my bedroom wall as a little girl. Astronomy is another field I'm interested in."

I was starting to enjoy this conversation. "What I love about that picture is that there are no borders, fences, or lines in the sand dividing us. What is so firm on maps and in our minds is so arbitrary. Our demarcations really don't exist when seen from space, outside our narrow, nationalistic focus. And I never could understand racism," I continued, "if you have just one tree in a forest, a disease can come along and wipe out the entire woods, but if you have a mix of trees and races, no way. There is strength in diversity. That's why I like New York City—every culture is here and for the most part people are learning to get along."

"London is that way, too. That's why so many people of color live there."

"I've never been to England, but I love how the Brits speak."

"You mean the accents?"

"Yes, but also their common usage of the language is so different than ours. The Dean of Science at Columbia where I studied and taught is from England. He calls a car trunk a *boot*, a flashlight a *torch*…"

"To kiss is to *snog*," Devi added.

"Really? Never heard him use that one before. *Snog*…sounds like something you blow into a Kleenex."

"And *fanny*, totally opposite meaning across the pond. Be careful with that one," Devi warned.

"Why?"

"Here in the States, *fanny* means backside, but in England it means a woman's vagina."

"Yikes."

"So, don't go slapping a British woman on her *fanny*," she laughed.

"Thanks for the tip." I bit into the sandwich. "Hey, Devi," I mumbled with my mouth full.

"Hey, what?"

"From your training," I paused to chew, "please tell me something men don't know about women."

"You mean sex?"

"Anything," I said, holding the container of olives out to her.

She thought for a moment as she bit into a spicy orb. "Somewhere on your body you have the mark of a woman."

"What?"

"Starting out all fetuses are female in the womb. Female is the default sex. Then about week six, if the male Y chromosome is present, testosterone floods in and male genitalia starts growing. But before that, the medium raphe line is already in place for the female vagina. If testosterone is present, the line doesn't go in, but is pushed out on the front of the scrotal sack and perineum but it's still there on a male—marking him for life."

"Wow. So the Bible, the Book of Genesis is wrong. Woman isn't made from man; it's the other way around."

"Precisely," she smiled, "and further proof is that men have nipples… totally useless…a carryover from starting out female."

I stood up to stretch my legs. "Tell me more about testosterone. It always gets such a bum rap. Deserving?"

"I don't know. I think testosterone and estrogen are just what they are: chemicals that evolution developed to keep the human race alive especially in early history. But their effects are very different." She reached for more olives. "Men experience that flood of testosterone twice in their lives. Around week six like I said and then at puberty…a really big surge then. Testosterone fuels male aggression, competitiveness, and risk-taking. Estrogen contributes to female nurturing and nesting. What's that saying? There's a jingle the professor told us.... Oh, yeah: *Testosterone makes the male prone to roam; estrogen, the woman prone to home.*"

"I'm not sure men and women can ever really get along," I sighed, sitting back down. "With all of our differences it seems totally improbable. I don't know any happy marriages and so many seem to end around six or seven years, over and over again. With sixty percent of married couples getting divorced and half cheating, I think either the whole system is broken or we're going about it all wrong. You wouldn't buy a stock that fails that often, yet we keep getting married. And why is it that more lying goes on with sex than any other area in human life? Why such deceit from decent people?"

Devi shrugged. "And what's really sad is that half of all children are sleeping in a home tonight where their father doesn't live."

"Do your parents have a good marriage?"

"It was arranged. And strangely they have somehow made it work. But they make it sound so cold and clinical, like it's a business deal. In India they think it's foolish to base something as important as a lifelong partnership on fleeting romantic love. And they want to do the same for me. They're always inviting me over for dinner with some new guy they picked out after a thorough financial interrogation. But it never seems to work out."

"Why not?"

"Indian men, even the younger generation, are very domineering and I can't stand being bossed around. One of the reasons I want to be a doctor is to have my own money and control my own life. But what about your parents, Michael?"

"They're dead."

"Oh, sorry."

"Car accident."

"Did they have a good marriage?" She touched my arm. "Don't talk about it if it's painful."

"It's OK. Yes, well sort of. I know my dad had a girlfriend on the side or girlfriends. He was a big, handsome guy with this radiant life force and interest in everything. He was a professor of philosophy at Columbia. He had so much charisma that he was magnetic. Women were drawn to him constantly. One time I came home from school early because I got sick and heard strange noises coming from his study. When I looked in, he was with a young woman."

"One of his students?"

"Here, try the cheesecake," I said, sliding a slice over to her. "She had been one of his students, had graduated—but who knows if it was the first time. After she left we went out for a walk and he told me he loved my mother, but that there was a difference between love and sex. *Sex is physical appetite*, he said. *Love is in the soul*."

"Did you tell your mother?"

"I think she knew. They were just so great together, made for each other, and I think she didn't want to leave because of me. So, that's why I'm not very hopeful and confused."

"Confused? About what?"

"Because he was so right about everything else. He was a great man. It was like he couldn't separate his passion for life from his passion for women—like one feeds the other. I want to prove my father wrong—get married and stay faithful. But then just walking down the street I lust after every beautiful woman I see! Add being raised Catholic to the mix—twelve years under the control of nuns and priests who hammered into my head that everything sexual is a sin. *Conflicted* is an understatement."

"And now you, Mister Bachelor, have thousands of women beating a path to your door—and bed!"

"The Catholic Church says that sex before marriage is a mortal sin."

"Well, somebody's about to get excommunicated…or have to go to confession four or five times a day! Oh, you must tell me how all this turns out. I read your Alaska book. Are you writing about your *Cosmo* experiences?

"Trying to."

"I'll buy the first copy. In the issue of *Cosmo* that you're in, there's an article that says men mate in their minds an average of seven times a day or two-thousand five-hundred and fifty-five times a year. In the same article as part of a psychology study conducted on a college campus an attractive young woman walked up to men and asked them if they wanted to go off and have sex. Ten out of ten men said yes. Then a good looking guy asked ten women. Only one was agreeable and she changed her mind on the way to the dorm."

"See," I shook my head slowly. "Should we blame it on testosterone?"

"I don't know. I think we became civilized too fast and now try to cram the sex drive into the tight confines of moralistic boxes, and the limbic, animal brain under the neocortex is rebelling. You can't eliminate millions of years of evolution in just a few centuries."

"What would you do if you caught your boyfriend or husband cheating?"

"Whip out a scalpel." Devi moved her watch toward a candle. "I have to get back to my shift. I enjoyed this. Thank you, Michael. You are very different than I expected."

"Really? How so?"

"I thought you would be stuck-up. But you are the opposite: very open and real."

"My father always said: *A man wrapped up in himself makes a small package.*"

"Before you go would you mind if we find someone to take our picture together? It's the only way my mother will believe that I met you."

Devi stopped a nurse in the hallway. She pulled a small camera out of her lab coat and handed it to her. I turned Devi's face toward me and snogged her good.

Back at my apartment, I opened my laptop and jumped on the internet to do some further research on human genetics, then wrote:

*THEOREM #2: Y THE X*

The male Y chromosome is a weird one. It only contains seventy-eight genes, far fewer than the female X strand, and sixty of the seventy-eight genes are devoted to sperm production, leaving just eighteen to influence everything else male. By our very DNA males are set up to be sex machines. Men aren't pigs. We're just primarily programmed to rut. So dominant is the sex drive in males, if women get anything else out of us they should consider it a bonus.

Reminds me of that country song: *I'm Living Up to Her Low Expectations.* Men deep down are really hoping, *She Thinks My Tractor's Sexy.*

And maybe females being the default sex live longer and have more developed brains—are able to handle more activity simultaneously and are better wired to have harmony between both cerebral lobes because they grow in the womb as constants—all of a set piece—without the tumultuous storm of testosterone flooding in for the re-form of turning female into male.

Two dates so far and both very different, yet the same in one respect. I found talking with Devi as stimulating as having sex with Shareen. When my mind is aroused, when I'm learning new things and having a great conversation, it is truly *intercourse* (the first definition in the dictionary is: *Dealings or communications between persons or groups.* Definition two is: *Sexual intercourse.*)

Intercourse is derived from the past participle of Latin *intercurrere*, meaning to mingle with. So, a mingling of the minds is as exciting to me as a tingling in the loins (gawd, a word Rathbone would use). But…being totally honest I don't think I could be married to Devi for as stimulating as our conversations would be I, like most males, am a slave to physical beauty…hopelessly/helplessly sight-driven.

I sense this is genetically embedded in the Y chromosome. It's as if our biological drive—the urge to merge—doesn't care if we're happy. It only cares if we merge and thus bombards the male with constant *alerts* to perform Job Number One.

# 6

# Dzunukwa

On a sunny late-autumn afternoon I went for a run, a wild leg and lung pumping ramble through the forested corridors of Central Park. Like a starved man I flung myself all out down every verdant path that presented itself. The trees still held most of their leaves with only a few starting to change colors. I recalled reading that chlorophyll and human blood are nearly identical substances that differ by only a single atom. I ran on smiling as my heart beat green with patches of red and gold.

In the depths of the park the wind gusted. I slowed and then stopped, turning an ear into the breeze. I heard something that took me back to Alaska, to another unseasonably warm day when I burst out of the cabin, bare-chested and kilt-clad.

Every time I wrapped the wool tartan around my waist with the green field drawn through with white and red, I paid homage to one of my heroes and distant ancestors, Sir Alexander Mackenzie, the first person to cross the continent of North America in 1793, twelve years before the Lewis & Clark Expedition. U.S. President Jefferson fully-funded Lewis and Clark's exploratory army; Alexander Mackenzie crossed the continent solo, rag-tag, and on the fly with his own limited resources.

Striding deeper into Central Park wearing regular running clothes, I made a mental note to wear the kilt more often. As I strode on, my mind returned to that Alaskan day of running, following a trail on the island into the northern rainforest. An eagle lifted from its perch and flew overhead leading me on. Following the eagle, I took a new path that led away from the coast into the center of the wilderness island. Stunned by the lush, fecund richness of the ancient forest I stopped running to soak it in. The gigantic plants, bushes and trees were so green they seemed to emit their own light. Suddenly the tree branches started stirring in the wind. As the treetops blew about, sunlight shafted down. The wind increased and the forest pulsed with strobic lances of light. I felt disoriented and dizzy.

Alone for years and somehow still alive after surviving so many life-or-death situations I was attuned to the deepest levels of nature, living more as instinctual animal than rational man. Then I heard a strange sound like tiny bells being shaken. The chiming persisted rising into eerie, high-pitched laughter. As I began to back away from where I stood I didn't see looming behind me the enormous cedar totem of a female goddess with pursed lips, bared breasts, and outstretched arms. Backing up, I slammed into her torso and her arms dropped down around me. The wooden visage groaned as I struggled frantically to break free.

I sprinted flat-out and dove into the cabin shaken to the core. A full moon later I heard an unfamiliar sound, the far off drone of a motorboat growing louder. I watched it make the turn into the bay. I walked out of the cabin and onto the beach with a pounding heart. I looked down at my tattered clothes and smoothed back my long hair. *Hope they won't think I'm a Sasquatch way out here.*

The small boat slowed, then the driver cut the power. I caught the bow and guided the boat to a stop on the beach sand. A dark-skinned native woman with silver hair stepped out. I stared at her wide-eyed. The physical presence of another person was overwhelming after so long alone. I opened my mouth to say hello, but the word fell apart on my tongue.

"Not good to be alone so long," the woman said, peering deep into my eyes. "Make it easy on yourself. Just think instead of talk and I'll hear you there."

*What?* I wondered.

Then a moment later inside my head I heard the woman say, "*If you are a Sasquatch, you clean up pretty good.*"

My head snapped back. *This can't be happening.*

*"Testing—one, two, three, four...."*

I clearly heard it in my brain. *"Who are you?"* I thought back.

*"Lucy."*

*"How are you doing this?"*

*"Found your frequency and tuned in..."* She glanced around at the forest and sea and back to me.

I was suddenly thrilled and no longer afraid. Her mere presence comforted me. I felt a deep peace.

*"...you have something to show me?"*

I knew exactly what she wanted to see. I led her along the trail I had taken to the center of the island. Lucy walked up to the statue standing guard over the forest. She reached out her hand and touched the totem's lowered hand reverently.

*"Dzunukwa,"* she said in my head.

She stood before Her and bowed her head as if listening. I sat back on a boulder. After a long minute Lucy walked over to me staggering a bit as if exhausted, but her eyes were shining bright. *"Took all I know to lift to her level."*

*"You mean that statue talked to you?"*

*"Not the statue. The spirit within."* She looked at me, disappointed. *"There is Spirit in everything. The essential is invisible to the eyes. Spirits,"* she extended her arms, *"are everywhere here, as you should know."*

As we walked back down the trail, she explained that Dzunukwa was the most powerful female earth spirit and the Goddess of the North Wind; that She was here and had taken up residence on my island for a reason.

*"Which is?"*

She just smiled. We walked along the beach and she pointed up at a lofty symmetrical spruce. *"Unlike man, no tree has branches that fight among themselves."* We stopped to admire wild flowers. *"Flowers are one of the highest forms of life for they give us such beauty, without asking anything in return. If only man would do the same, give more than he takes, the world would be a better place."*

She told me everything she knew about killer whales and I scribbled it all down after receiving her permission to add it as a postscript to my book. I told her about seeing them paint with plankton, bioluminescence in the ocean at night in Blackfish Fjord, and how if the first sign of intelligence in a species is how well they live in harmony with their environment, then the whales and dolphins were light years ahead.

Lucy nodded. *"Every animal knows more than you do. The animals are better than us. They exist in a constant state of love, free of deceit, and are on a higher plane. Man is stuck in the mud, wanting things he doesn't need and viewing the world through a prison of arrogance and alienation. Man is now homeless, in exile from Nature, and, therefore, his own true self. It's why he acts so crazy and Nature is a mirror reflecting back that sickness. All things are bound together, but man has broken the sacred bond."* She raised one hand and opened her palm; the other hand she placed over my heart. *"The Nature around you is the Nature within you. Where you live is who you are."*

I stopped walking. *"That's what I feel every day out here. Sometimes I feel so close to it, at one with it all that it feels like if I open my mouth—the land and sea will come pouring out!"*

Lucy's eyes flashed up at me and she smiled.

As we walked on, I asked something I had long been struggling with: *"What is the best way to live and love?"*

*"The best way to live and love?"* Without looking up, she pointed to the sky. *"Watch an eagle riding the wind."* Where there was empty sky, we now watched an eagle soaring—the wind filling his wings. *"He's in the perfect flow of the Universe...."*

In the early evening after dinner, we built a fire on the beach and sat staring at the flames, going long stretches without talking telepathically, which I no longer questioned. It felt as natural and effortless as breathing. I was deeply relaxed and content to simply bask in her presence.

*"You are about to leave here,"* she finally said in my head.

*"Really?"* My shoulders slumped. *"Just as I feared. That's why I sent the book out, my manuscript, adrift in the skiff—to stay here forever or at least buy more time. Did you find it?"*

*"Yes."*

*"Was the money still there with the manuscript to mail it?"*

*"Yes."*

*"Did you read the book before you—"*

*"Yes."*

*"What did you think?"*

She picked up a stick and stirred the fire. *"Not bad for a white man."*

I smiled.

*"The real reason you are leaving is not the book."*

*"It isn't?"*

*"You are leaving because your soul is not fully formed. You have developed your male side, but now you need the female to be complete. A man finds his way to Nature and his own true self through Woman. Out here you have been put to many tests and have passed them all or Dzunukwa wouldn't be so pleased with you. She knows you have treated her creatures with love and respect. Your soul has learned from this world and grown deep. She is ready to reward you, but...."*

*"But what?"*

Lucy stared into the flames. *"With this gain comes great risk. You are about to enter a jungle far more dangerous than this one."*

*"More dangerous than wrestling a cougar or fending off a grizzly bear?"*

She waved her hand dismissively. *"More dangerous for your emotions will be involved."*

*"Where am I going?"*

She pulled an envelope from her jacket and held it up to the firelight. *"New York City."*

Did I now hear in Central Park the chiming of tiny bells and the same windy laughter from Dzunukwa? I ran on—toward something now rather than away from it.

***

I accepted an invitation to lecture at the New York Zoological Society (now known as the World Conservation Society), followed by a book signing. As I showered and dressed for the event, I felt relieved to have an opportunity to get back to my roots, turn my attention away from women to whales. The audience of about a hundred people was older and conservative. I talked from the stage spontaneously awhile, read an excerpt from my book, and then voiced over a film of the killer whales in action—feeding, breaching, and mating.

As the males thrashed about, their three-foot long, pink penises heaving into view, I commented on the lack of pair-bonding in cetacean society. The gigantic sperm cannons flailed wildly across the screen. The elderly women gasped, their eyeglasses reflecting the horrifying spectacle of the blubbery orgy. My comments were drowned in the aqueous churning. Attempting to inject some humor into the proceedings, I added an impromptu audio footnote that everyone unfortunately heard, "The male whale's penis is referred to as a *Pink Floyd.* The origin of this term is not known, but legend has it that groupies of the rock band Pink Floyd were paying homage to the band members' sizeable *members.*"

When the presentation was over, the applause was meager, except for one young woman who slapped her hands together enthusiastically. After I had signed a few books, I looked up and saw the young woman standing before me.

"Ellen Klein," she said, extending her hand. "I totally agree with what you said. I'm an anthropologist with a minor in zoology. Human society would be better off if we were more like the dolphins and whales…doing without social contracts and artificial, moral constrictions."

As we walked out of the theater together to the street, I felt an immediate attraction. Ellen was tall and leggy with long dark hair and she exuded intelligence.

"I'm famished," she said. "Let's have dinner. After your show, I want to sink my teeth into some thick, juicy meat. Have you eaten?"

"No."

She lifted an arm and a taxi screeched to a halt. We went to Smith & Wollensky. Inside the carnivore cathedral, I picked up the oversized, custom-made steak knife that dominated my plate setting. "Nahw, thot's a *knauiiife!*"

"Not bad, Crocodile Dundee."

She ordered the crackling pork shank with firecracker applesauce. I went with a sirloin topped with caramelized onions.

"Mind if I pick the wine?" she said.

"Please." I handed over the massive, leather-bound book.

"Good, they have it." She ordered a '96 Bonny Doon Zinfandel. "And some appetizers, please. Field mushrooms on toast. Are the oysters fresh?"

"Yes," the waiter said smugly. "That's the only way we serve them."

"Where are they from?" she tested him.

"Hogg Island, Pt. Reyes, California…flown in this morning."

"Excellent," Ellen said, snapping the menu shut. She then leaned toward me. "Hope you don't think I'm a pig."

"No," I grinned. "Good to see a woman with an appetite. My previous girlfriend, whenever we went out, she'd eat a lettuce leaf and a baby carrot."

"Yeah and then went home and stuffed herself silly."

I liked her candor and sass.

The waiter returned with the wine. After Ellen tasted and nodded her assent and the waiter filled our glasses with the velvety red libation, I examined the bottle. The label was a wild drawing: a loose satirical scrawl of a Catholic clergy man with CARDINAL ZIN across the top. "Great label."

Ellen nodded. "Done by Ralph Steadman, the Gonzo artist. Check out Bonny Doon's website sometime. Their slogan is *Go forth and Zin some more*."

I smiled.

"So," she continued, "how does it feel to be a *Cosmo* Bachelor?"

I dropped my head.

"What?"

"I thought you wanted to hear about Alaska, not me."

A toothy grin. "I read everything. I probably bought the first copy of your book, then the copy of *Cosmo* came in, and then the Zoological Society newsletter, saying you were speaking. I put two and two or three together and know what else?"

"What?" I said, feeling a bit uneasy.

"I wrote to you to the address in *Cosmo.* But you haven't called." Her bottom lip curled and eyelashes fluttered. "Boo-hoo."

We both laughed.

After the feast, I watched in amazement as Ellen quickly put away a milk chocolate crème brulé. "Good to be home again," she said.

"Where did you go?"

"Tanzania. Three weeks with the Maasai and eating only what they eat, curdled milk and cow's blood. I'm doing my Ph.D. dissertation on them and hope to be finished by spring. Needed one more trip to wrap things up."

"Wow. Sounds great."

"Your Bachelor thing isn't much different than what each Maasai male goes through for a few years. In their youth, the *morani* or warriors are free to roam the land and whoop it up with all the women they want. And unlike our society with its double-slut standard some tribal African women enjoy fair play."

"How so?"

"While a husband is off traveling a wife may have other lovers, up to three. They even have names: the first is called the *Sweetheart* for whom she prepares milk; second is called the *Skewer*, for obvious reasons and he takes over when the first is not around; third is *The One Who Crosses Over* and he may court her favors when the other two are gone. However, in her fertile times she will only sleep with her husband as to ensure that the children are his. Native Africans tend to view sex as a natural appetite without attaching the religious guilt restrictions that we do. Their attitude is that if you feel hungry, you eat," she said, licking the last streaks of chocolate off the spoon. "And if you're horny, you fuck. Living close to nature, they pattern themselves after the birds and animals, which are mostly polygamous, monogamy being the minority in the natural world."

"Was it just me or did you notice how shocked those little old ladies in the audience were by the killer whales' mating?"

"Next time quote Mark Twain, *Nature has no indecencies; man invents them.*"

When the check came, I saw that it was close to two hundred dollars. Ellen snatched it out of my hand. "My treat."

"No way. Let's at least spli…"

"Enjoy it while it lasts, Michael Morani...."

Outside on the street, I thanked her for the evening.

"Instead of inviting you up to see my etchings, want to see my collection of primitive art?" Ellen asked. "I even have some pieces from your neck of the woods, Tlingit and Kwakiutl."

"Great. Let's go."

# 7

# MICHAEL MORANI

The cab stopped in front of an elegant building on Park Avenue. A doorman dashed out to greet "Ms. Klein." A private elevator whisked us up to the penthouse. A butler opened the door. Ellen asked for two brandies. I walked over and stood before a wall of tall windows, drinking in the view. Around the dark, tree-filled island of Central Park, New York City glittered and gleamed. "Wow. Feels like flying. This is yours?"

"Yes. My great grandfather invented the light bulb."

"Thought that was Edison."

"No, he made electricity workable. The Klein kin got the first patent on practical application. Caught lightning in a bottle so to speak."

As I took my eyes from shimmering New York to look around the penthouse, I was very impressed.

In the main living room, Ellen showed me the art: New Guinea ancestor statues with piercing cowrie-shell eyes; West African Voodun gods and goddesses infused with the oldest, root religion on earth; a *Nkondi* from Togo, wearing a blizzard of nails to release spiritual power and a small mirror in the navel, deflecting evil spirits; and abstract, dual-perspective masks from Burkina Faso that preceded Picasso's cubism by a thousand years. There was a Northwest Coast Raven mask with a three-foot long, tapered wooden beak that clacked open and shut when Ellen tugged on a concealed string, and Maasai shields chipped and chewed from lion attacks and decorated in patterns that redefined geometry. The aged wood and muted colors were set off perfectly by grey matte walls and chrome-trimmed leather furniture, and the pieces were spot-lit from recessed lighting concealed in the ceiling.

She led me into the library. There were hundreds of primitive art books and first edition, steel-engraved, leather bound sets from the early explorers. The solid walls of books were interrupted throughout the room with exquisite Zulu baskets and Navajo bowls.

A small room off the library served as Ellen's study. The desk was a stateroom door that floated up from the Titanic. I sank into a leather chair and looked over a sleek computer to the lone painting in the room: *The Dream* by Henri Rousseau.

"Original?" I inquired.

She nodded. "Daddy's. On temporary loan to me for inspiration. After I finish my Ph.D., it goes back to the Met where it's on permanent display."

I strolled over and stood reverently before it. The naked woman reclining on the red velvet sofa surrounded by lush jungle made my heart sing.

"Come on," she said.

She took me to her bedroom. The bed was an antique, mahogany four-poster, deeply-carved with fleur-de-lis. "It belonged to Madame Du Châtelet, the mistress of Voltaire. The most famous courtesan of her day and as smart as she was beautiful. She translated Newton's *Principia Mathematica* into French." A canopy of porous white drapes engulfed the bed. "It's mosquito netting," Ellen said, fluffing back the light fabric so we could peer in. "This way I have both worlds at once: camping in luxury."

"Like floating on a cloud," I said, looking around inside the white cocoon.

Straightening up, I did a double-take. On the walls on each side of the doorway were at least fifty penises standing on shelves at full attention.

"A donation from each of my lovers," she said.

The blood left my face.

Ellen laughed. "You thought I was serious! Silly Morani."

Walking closer, I saw most were carved from wood. Many were huge. "My lingam collection. *Lingam* is the Hindi word for cock; as *yoni* is for cunt. I collected them from all around the world, but mostly from India, Bhutan, and rural Japan. Those cultures don't have all the hang-ups we do about sex. They're displayed out in the open and the big ones are used in fertility ceremonies usually in the spring. This one's from Bhutan," Ellen, pausing to pick up an imposing red pecker said, "Up in the high Himalayas. Hard place to get to."

She turned it over horizontally. "Most frightening flight in commercial aviation. Fewer than a dozen pilots know how to get in." She lifted the penis and moved it through the air. "It requires a tight right turn at Mt. Everest, then a steep slide down to the airstrip at 10,000 feet." The descending penis landed in my hands.

"Whoa," I grimaced.

"Don't worry, it won't bite."

"Just feels strange, holding *wood* not my own."

She laughed.

We left the bedroom and walked down a long hallway, stopping in front of a door. "Through there is Jeeves' quarters."

"Is that really his name?"

"No, it's Randolph. But ever since I was a little girl, I've called him Jeeves and it stuck. He likes it. Takes the edge off. He's been with the family forever and does everything."

Back in the main room, Jeeves was standing with two brandies in globe snifters on a silver tray. "Ah, there you are," he beamed at Ellen.

"Thank you, Randolph," she said as we took up the brandies.

He looked crestfallen. "Madame is mad at me?"

"No, just proving a point. Thank you, Jeeves. We'll be fine the rest of the evening."

"Very well." He smiled as he walked away.

We sat and sipped the brandy. I felt as if I was in a dream and told Ellen as much.

"Why do you feel that way?"

"Well, it starts with you being an exceptional woman and then this extraordinary place." I paused to look around. "And all the primitive art with that deep other-worldly power, it takes me back to Alaska."

She flipped open a small silver box on a round table next to her. "Cigarillo?"

"No, thanks."

"Mind if I do?"

"Not at all."

She lit the dark brown stick, sucked a deep draw, then slowly exhaled a cloud of blue smoke. "What you just said and how you said it reminds me of how you were on stage tonight. You are very different when you talk about Alaska and the whales."

"How so?"

"Your passion is palpable. And passion is a polite word for *lust.*"

"Well, I think everyone has a geographical place where they feel most at home, most alive. Alaska is *IT* for me."

"Then what are you doing here?"

"Selling my book, and I'm on somewhat of a quest."

"A quest?"

I told her about Lucy, the native elder and her prediction, and about the plan to study women as I had the wildlife.

"So, are you finding it more *dangerous* here?"

"Yes, I feel I'm in uncharted waters and way over my head. I never had much luck with women before and now to be this *Bachelor*—in all honesty I feel overwhelmed."

She pursed her lips and puffed a smoke ring that expanded across the room encircling me. "Do you want to be my lover?"

I nearly spat a mouthful of brandy at her. Struggling to hold it back the alcohol crashed and burned against my gullet. *"Whaa?"* I gasped, with a red, twisted face.

"I ask for two reasons. One, I'm attracted to you. Atop the scientific nerd, Alaska gave you a raw, animal magnetism. Two, you've lived in quarantine for the last five years so AIDS for the most part is out of the equation. If you got it before you left for

Alaska, you'd be dead by now or at least showing signs. And you *do* use protection with all the *Cosmo* girls?"

I nodded, struggling to regain my speech as the held-back brandy fumed in my nose and throat.

"I believe in full disclosure and total honesty at all times; if women and men had the courage to be that way with each other all the misery would cease."

"Ellen, I would be honored to be your lover. But...."

She dropped the smoking cigarillo into an ashtray and leaned forward. "I'm not asking for exclusivity. This is your time, Morani—time for a warrior to have his way."

Ellen stood up, walked over, and extended her hand. I placed my hand in hers, and she led me into the bedroom.

***

Two days later, I limped back to my apartment. I paused in front of a mirror and saw a look of amazed delight plastered across my face. If my prehensile tail was still evident, it would be wagging back and forth and thumping on the floor. At my desk, I powered up the laptop and wrote:

*THEOREM #3: SACRED SEX*

It began with the *Kama Sutra* that Ellen propped up on a pillow at the head of the bed; the binding spiral-ringed like a cookbook so we could reach out and flip the pages. Nineteen down. Five hundred and ten positions to go! Following this ancient guide to carnal contortions, we did The Pestle, The Cobra, The Conch, The High Squeeze, The Black Bee....

And in true, poetic Hindu tradition, we agreed that henceforth we would refer to the male organ as *The Crimson Bird* and the female sex, *The Cinnabar Grotto.* Although, at one point, when I was at full breach, Ellen called it a "Pink Floyd" and wondered if the gigantic appendage could possibly fit inside the Grotto. Great for my ego, though hardly the truth. Call it what you may, *The Crimson Bird*, *Pink Floyd*, or *The North Pole*—I was inspired to new heights.

Then after the *Kama Sutra* warm-up, Ellen said: "Men know how to tune up a car, but don't know the first thing about turning on a woman. Want to learn?"

I nodded eagerly. She took control and schooled me in exactly how she liked to be touched. It was electrifying!

"When you touch my skin, where a hundred erogenous zones reside" (the *K. Sutra* influencing even our conversation) "do it as lightly as possible, so lightly that there is air between your fingers and my skin. By levitating your fingers above the skin, they brush these fine body hairs…*antennas* in the electrical field…triggering shivers up my spine and unlocking my chakras." Ellen said that predictability takes away from pleasure. Stopping and restarting a touch or thrust, coming at her in an assortment of ways, builds and intensifies the previous sensation.

So with a clear channel of honest, no ego communication open between us, I attempted to play many instruments in the sexual orchestra with varying rhythms and speeds and to my surprise the results were spectacular! Is there any greater satisfaction upon this earth than for a man to feel a woman's body build to crescendos and hear her love songs time and time again erupt in your ear? Maybe there's hope for me yet…hope that someday I can be a great lover under the tutelage of a superb conductor like Ellen Klein.

During the two nights and days we spent together in bed, we stopped only for a few, simple raw foods: figs, pine nuts, dark chocolate (antioxidants, all), and oysters for me. Zinc keeps up male strength. (Seems Casanova downed sixty of the slippery fripperies a day.) And sticks of fresh celery for her. Celery, Ellen explained, contains androsterone, the male hormone that feeds sexual arousal in females. CELERY? Who knew? All washed down with a couple bottles of tangy Zins (the tannic acid in red wine absorbing toxins and oxygenating the heart and blood).

Ellen has it down to both art and science. She's an anthropologist of exotic, arcane eroticisms and an incredibly fit sexual marathoner. And the sex went against everything brainwashed into me being brought up Catholic. Deep in the throes of passion, late the first day, there was a tipping point, where instead of sex being sinful or dirty, what we did glowed with sacredness and divinity, so much so that it dissolved normal reality and I went away to a white-light place, far removed, yet sparked by our animal passions where total peace and harmony and the deepest of satisfactions prevailed.

And so amazing how a woman's legs seem to *unhinge* and lay out near-horizontal to the sides. What author Henry Miller called, *The Rosy Crucifixion.*

Then toward the end, when the sheets were soaked and we were spent, seemingly more spirits than bodies, something happened that totally blew my mind…that I'm still trying to recover from and come to terms with. Ellen was on her back with her legs spread wide. I was doing cunnilingus when suddenly she rocked back and something deep within the Cinnabar Grotto quaked open and there was a gush of the sweetest tasting liquid that hit my tongue and lit up all the sensors in my soul like a pinball machine!

After coming down from what Ellen said was a tantric orgasm, she explained that I hit her G-spot and the fluid is called *Amrita.* When a woman deeply relaxes and expands her consciousness during sex, she said, she becomes a gateway to the cosmic forces that created the Universe. And that sex is holy, a re-enactment of the divine union of the god Shiva and goddess Shakti. Amrita is the nectar of the gods, and resides in the bodies of women.

Ellen said that vaginal fluid is full of hormones, such as prostaglandins, highly venerated by ancient, enlightened cultures and said to contain properties for healing and magic. In China, yoni fluid is believed to be the fountain of youth. Supposedly, Chairman Mao's aged virility was restored when he sipped from the *cups* of virgins.

After touting all the natural benefits of sex, Ellen said, "If there was a drug that could do all these beneficial things, everybody would buy it, and yet it's built right into our bodies, hard-wired in all of us, but because of religious repression we denigrate sex instead of celebrating it."

Something I've sensed for a long time, I'm now certain about: there's something very wrong with the way we view sex. With religions teaching that God is separate from man… and the toll to cross that bridge extracted in corrupt collection baskets every Sunday…we know nothing. For two straight days and nights, I worshipped in awe directly at the Altar of Woman—the Cunt Cathedral. For the first time I was on my knees and truly in touch with the Divine.

Googling the *C word* today, I learned that what our society considers to be the worst thing to call a woman now was the opposite of an insult long ago in wiser times when goddess energy ruled the earth. Before the patriarchal take over when men tried to control females in every way, even renaming the part of a woman that most obsessed them *vagina,* meaning: *the sheath of a sword.* Talk about self-serving.

The word *cunt* is derived from the goddess Kali's title of Cunti, and shares the same root with *kin* and *country*. And from *The Women's Encylopedia of Myths and Secrets* by Barbara G. Walker, "In ancient writings, the word for *cunt* was synonymous with *woman* though not in the insulting modern sense. An Egyptologist was shocked to find the maxims of Ptah-Hotep used a term for *woman* that was more than blunt, though its indelicacy was not in the eye of the ancient beholder but only in that of the modern scholar."

Women, reclaim thy cunts! Let's return to the days, I say, when *cunt* was a compliment and prostitutes were priestesses. One thousand of them at The Temple of Aphrodite in Corinth in the sixth century teaching that the most sacred thing a man could do in this life was to learn how to fuck.

And it's no coincidence that churches are designed like cunts. From an essay by Gloria Steinem, "In the 1970's, while researching in the Library of Congress, I found an obscure history of religious architecture that assumed a fact as if it were common knowledge: the traditional design of most patriarchal buildings of worship imitates the female body. Thus, there is an outer and inner entrance, labia majora and labia minora; a central vaginal aisle toward the altar; two curved ovarian structures on either side; and then at the sacred center, the altar or womb...."

I feel such a rush of happiness now. I laugh for no reason. Colors look brighter. I can almost see through walls, and could if I had another shot of Amrita. Erotic energy is not just about having sex. It is life energy. It's what it means to be fully alive. And it takes the sexual into the spiritual—reuniting the two. If sex isn't sacred and a woman's cunt doesn't connect us directly to the Divine, then why did I instinctually shout, "OH GOD! OH GOD!" all the while with Ellen?

The Gates of Heaven are here on earth.

# 8

# Ben Wa

## Ellen Klein

**Species Name**: *Aphroditi Libertinus*

**Habitat & Range:** Temples of Greece, Japan, China, Africa, and American Sports Bars

**Identifying Characteristics:** Aggressive behavior in courtship

**Best Known For:** Polyandrous (mating with more than one male)

Ellen called early the next morning, "Hey, I have two surprises for you. Can you come over tonight?"

"Surprises? You mean there's MORE? I'm still recovering from the last session."

"Oh, we're just getting started."

"More Kama Sutra?"

"No, much better."

Curiosity piqued, I agreed to be there at eight. Jeeves answered the door.

"Ms. Klein is waiting for you in the bedroom."

I grinned sheepishly and knocked at the bedroom door.

"Entre vous."

I walked into the darkened bedroom. Ellen, who had been hiding behind the door, stepped out behind me and placed her hands over my eyes. "Keep them closed," she said. I felt a blindfold encircle my head. I reached up and touched a silk scarf that she knotted at the back of my neck.

She took my hand and led me over to the bed. Already naked, she kissed me, and then took off my clothes. I stood at full attention. "Now lie on the bed, on your back in the center."

Hands out, feeling my way, I did as I was told. She climbed up on the end of the bed, then stood up, the bed bouncing slightly as she stepped forward, legs apart, until her feet were on each side of my waist. "Keep your hands in at your sides." She then reached down, grasped my erection and guided it inside of her. I moaned, then murmured: "Oh God—I feel you there, but where's the rest of you?"

"Lift your hands. Feel the rope on both sides?"

"Yesss."

"Now move me. Not back and forth, but around and around."

I did as instructed and the sensation was out of this world. Neurons and dangling ganglia fired for the first time along new pleasure paths, igniting my brain like never before. I quickly got the hang of it, spinning Ellen around in tight circles as I stayed inside of her. Then I alternated directions—until the top of my head felt like it was going to explode.

"But what about you? I. Want to. Please—*you!*"

"Don't worry about me. This is for you, Morani—all for you...."

With both hands on the braided rope, I gave it a final twist. She spun completely around on me as I bucked and thrashed to exquisite release.

Slowing, she caught the mattress with her feet. She flipped off my blindfold.

I looked up at her, dazed, shaken. "What—where did you get *that*?"

"Japanese spin-fuck chair," she said matter-of-factly. "You like?"

I followed the rope brocade up to a swivel hook in the ceiling. I nodded, and nodded some more.

She stepped out of the seat and lay down beside me. I slapped the empty rope around and around above us. "I'll never look at macramé the same way again." I kissed her and held her tight.

She got up and lit a cigarillo. "Ready for your next surprise?"

I sighed through a smile. "Don't know if I can handle any more."

She picked up a black box from the nightstand. I sat up on the edge of the bed. She opened the box. Nestled on black velvet were two small, gold balls. Ellen rolled the orbs suggestively in her hand.

"Not sure I want to ask where those go," I said, warily.

She lay back on a chair with her legs apart. Staring directly into my eyes, she inserted the balls into her cunt. She sat up and crossed one leg over the other. "Ben Wa balls from ancient China, but with a modern twist." She handed me a remote control.

"You've got to be kidding."

"No, try it. Here now, then we're going out."

I eyed the remote then tapped the button. Her eyes closed, eyelashes fluttered, and a blissful grin spread across her face. I dropped the remote on the bed as if it was a hot potato.

Her eyes snapped open. "What?"

I shook my head. "Ellen, I don't know about this. Not out in public."

"Come on. I gave you spin-fuck. You owe me Ben Wa."

I took a moment to process the exotic logic. "But why can't we just play here?"

"Because seeing if I can control myself—both feel and fend off the pleasure while surrounded by people in a public setting—that's the sexual charge." She took a long drag on the cigarillo and held it before exhaling the smoke. "When you were spinning me around, did you feel anything gripping and squeezing you?"

"Yeah, that's when you used your hand."

"No, I didn't."

"What?"

"Holding Ben Wa balls in on a regular basis, exercises and tightens the Kegel muscles. Ancient Chinese practice."

"You mean all the time that was your…"

"Uh-huh."

"Will you marry me?"

She burst into laughter.

"I don't know." I reached for her cigarillo, took a drag, and handed it back. "I want to stay in that Sacred Zone. Going out in public, well, it doesn't seem the same."

"The Sacred knows no bounds. It pushes the limits constantly. That's how the universe was created—by expanding outward. Hell is becoming predictable, stuck in a rut, doing the same thing over and over until *poof,"* she snapped her fingers, "sex collapses in on itself and disappears."

"Can I ask you something?"

"Shoot."

"You didn't have your first orgasm in a normal way, did you?"

"Nope," she grinned. "Had my first one at age eleven…at the zoo. It was feeding time in the lions' den. The many males with thick, musk-drenched, bushy manes all made explosions of wild sounds; thunderous roars that had me quivering and dripping wet. In Africa, a lion's roar can be heard five miles away and kicks up a cloud of dust."

"Where do you propose we go?"

"A sports bar. The World Series is on. I'm a big Yankees fan. And there's a dog in the bar that watches television."

"Are you sure he doesn't have a mane and weighs five hundred pounds?"

She rolled her eyes.

"Sure you can control yourself?"

"No," she said through a whiplash grin. "Let's find out."

Feeling both aroused and somewhat obligated, I stood up. I picked up the Ben Wa remote. "What's the range on this thing?"

"Fifty feet. You don't even have to be near me, and it might be more exciting if you're not. Then you can see my reactions."

"We going to be near any metal detectors?"

We got dressed. Against my better judgment, I pocketed the power control and we charged out the door.

Inside Max's Sports Bar, Ellen introduced me to Max, a bulldog wearing a New York Yankees cap, brim backwards. Max looked up at me warily with droopy, bloodshot eyes, and then enthusiastically licked Ellen's bare leg.

Ellen walked away and sat at a table facing me. I sat down at a table near the bar, slowly removed the remote control from my pocket and hid it on the top of my left thigh under the table. I tapped the button. Ellen smiled.

I was distracted by game seven of the World Series, on a half-dozen, flat-screen TVs on walls around the room. Feeling ignored, Ellen plucked a pen out of her purse and scribbled something on a napkin. She folded it in half; handed it to a waitress and pointed to me.

The waitress delivered the note with my beer. I read: *GIVE IT TO ME*! Just as I reached down to press the button, a crowd of people stormed in.

A young woman slammed into me and the remote fell to the floor as she blurted, "Ohmigod. Oh. My. God. You're him! I have my *Cosmo* in my purse. Would you please—oh, I can't believe this, like sign your picture for me?"

I glanced down to make sure the remote was out of harm's way. "Sure." As the woman swung a gigantic purse off her shoulder it bashed me squarely on the head. She excitedly whipped out her magazine and a pen.

While signing the magazine, I overheard a woman seated at the bar tell the bartender she was flying to Italy tomorrow and ask if she could switch over to the Weather Channel during the commercials to catch the temperature for Rome? The bartender handed her the one remote that controlled all the sets. "Make it quick and watch the slobber; it's Max's favorite toy."

"Eww," the woman said, channel surfing around dried bulldog spittle and coarse hairs.

Immediately, Max saw that something was amiss. He trotted to the bar and looked up at the bartender, who ignored him. He dropped his rumpled face to the floor and ran around, searching for his control. While I was preoccupied talking to the Cosmo girl, the bulldog found what he was looking for. I watched in horror as Max picked up the Ben Wa remote, strutted out to an open spot, dropped it, then lifted a paw and stomped on the button.

All hell broke loose at once. Rome's temperature appeared on the nearest screen. The woman called for the bartender. Not seeing sports on the screens, Max furrowed his brow even more, and jumped on the button with both paws. The traveler handed the doggy remote over with two fingers grasping a clean corner.

"HEY—WHERE'S THE BALLGAME?" someone shouted.

Beads of sweat rained down Ellen's brow.

The bartender clicked back to the World Series. "THERE'S A LONG DRIVE TO DEEP CENTER...." the announcer blasted.

Ellen's eyes rolled back in her head.

"IT'S GOING...."

She slid down to the floor.

"GOING! *GONNNNE!!*"

Flat on her back, Ellen erupted in a full-throated roar that was drowned in applause as everyone jumped to their feet shouting their approval at the screens. Max finally took his paws off the button and broke into a home run trot around the room.

She told me later that lightning forked behind her eyes and thunder rumbled down her legs, curling her toes.

# 9

# Plague Doctor

**<u>University Girls</u>**
**Species Name:** *Sorority Ifeltathi*
**Habitat & Range:** In the Land of Keggers
**Identifying Characteristics:** Mostly nocturnal. Peck at their food, but fond of fermented nectar that raises testosterone levels in the female-only flocks, resulting in unrestrained behavior.
**Best Known For:** Occasional flashing of bare breasts, or both wings raised overhead, with throaty calls of *WA-HOOO!*

The next morning, I called Ellen. She didn't answer. I left a message: "All I can say is thank goodness for the New York Yankees coming through with a homer in the bottom of the ninth. A reporter once said to The Yankee Clipper after he married Marilyn Monroe: 'So, Mr. DiMaggio, how does it feel to be an expert at two national pastimes?' This curious scribe now asks the same of you, Ms. Klein."

Later in the evening, returning from the gym, I saw that my home phone had one message. I hit play.

"Hey," Ellen said. "I've been in bed all day, can't move a muscle. Even my eyelashes are sore. Feels like I was turned inside-out. Everything has a weird pink glow around it. If men are dogs maybe that's not a bad thing…not a bad thing at all."

That night Steve called, "Get over to Mission Control quick! You've *got* to see this!!"

"What?" I said, jumping up from my desk at the sound of the runaway excitement in Steve's voice.

"But don't be you. It's Halloween. Wear a costume or something."

"What is it? What's going on?"

"Trick or treat, only all the *Treats* want YOU to be their *Trick*!"

"What?"

"Shut up and *GET OVER HERE.*"

I looked through my closet for some sort of costume, but all I saw were just plain clothes. Then I remembered the trunk on the floor of the closet, under the clothes. I pulled the trunk out into the bedroom, flipped the latch and lifted the top. Rummaging through the things I saved after my parents' deaths, I found the masks they'd brought back from Venice, Italy when they'd attended Carnival.

I lifted the female mask out first and it sent a chill down my spine. It was a replica of my mother's face: her exact beautiful features in alabaster white with ruby red lips and blazing blue-marble eyes topped by a jester's gold brocade, tri-pointed hat, with each downward sloping flange tipped with a tinkling silver bell. I set the mask down on the bed.

I took out the male mask and placed it on the bed next to my mother's. It was as ugly as mother's was beautiful: a stork-like face with a long, rigid beak. Folded, dark fabric in the trunk caught my eye. I lifted out a velvet cape, letting it fall open. I put it on and it was just my size. There was also a gold wand and a big, floppy black hat in the trunk. I placed the items on the bed next to the male mask and then turned the horrible visage over, looking for ties. Inside the hollow beak I saw a curled piece of paper. I unrolled it and recognized my father's handwriting. I read: *The Plague Doctor. This mask is the medieval doctor's face-protector (beak stuffed with a filter of straw). Worn with long, black cape and hat as protection against the Plague as he made his rounds treating patients.*

I lifted the mask to my face and secured it with the ties. I put on the hat and took up the wand. I picked up my mother's mask, held it to my heart for a moment, then placed it back, bells tinkling, into the trunk.

The Plague Doctor turned on his heel, cape swirling as he dashed out into the night. Approaching Rathbone's house, I heard female shrieking and wailing. When I turned the corner, I stopped dead in my tracks. Covering the front steps of Rathbone's brownstone, filling the sidewalks, and spilling out into the street were at least a hundred young women dressed in skimpy, sexed-up costumes. Many looked like Britney Spears, with Lindsay Lohans and a few Lil' Kims mixed in. Some went for the retro look, imitating Julia Roberts' *Pretty Woman* with micro-minis, thigh high boots, and tumbling, tangled tresses.

From the top of the front steps, Kwame frantically tossed handfuls of candy out to the crowd.

"We don't want candy. We want the real thing!"

"Yeah, we want Michael!"

Kwame shouted, "I TOLD YA—HE AIN'T HERE!"

"WE WANT MICHAEL! WE WANT MICHAEL!" The chant spread until they all were screaming it.

The Plague Doctor gulped and reached back to cinch his mask tighter. Spotting Steve in a tiger costume standing off to the side of the crowd, I sidled over to him. "Steve," I said, muffled through the mask: "It's me, Michael. What the hell is going on?"

"YOU'RE HERE!" Steve shouted, raising a half-empty bottle of scotch.

"*Shhhhhh.* What is all of this?"

"What da hell," Steve eyed me up and down, "you look like Doctor Doom. A sorority from Columbia; they all got liquored up at a *Bitches & Ho's* party and came looking for you. Don't they look *GRRREAT!*" He raised a striped paw and swiped it through the air.

"Where're Ralph and Rathbone?"

"Saw Ralph go upstairs with a bunch of Ho's. Rathbone is making drinks. You know him, always the perfect host."

"Oh, no."

Wailing police sirens cut the air and two squad cars turned the corner and slammed to a stop. The *Bitches & Ho's* dispersed—the Brittney Spears imitators escaping quickly in their schoolgirl skirts and saddle shoes, while the rest of the young women teetered away as fast as possible in skin-tight dresses and stiletto heels. I froze, standing statue-still, as a stream of young women wobbled by until one, catching a heel in a concrete crack, toppled into my arms.

The woman's eyes were swimming as she looked up at me and she reeked of tequila. "Killer costume!" Her hand whipped up, curled into a circle and stroked my elongated beak. The mask dropped down and the girl's eyes widened.

I stood her on her feet and cringing, turned away.

"ITZZ *HIMMM!!!*" she screamed at the top of her lungs.

The Plague Doctor strode away—slowly outdistancing the ladies of the night.

# 10

# Smashing

With my life spinning totally out of control, I retreated deep into my man cave, and stayed there for two days and nights, refusing all calls, e-mails, and letters. Eating delivered pizza and Chinese, I tried to escape reality by watching movie after movie. Finally able to fall asleep, I dreamed I was being stalked by the giantess from the film, *Attack of the 50 Ft. Woman.* She chased me through downtown Manhattan pushing over rigid skyscraper penises like rows of dominoes.

Fortunately, I was scheduled to get out of town. A collaborative effort between my agent, Liz and Rathbone had landed interviews with BBC Radio and TV in London to help promote my book. At the airport, I was nervous and edgy and hid behind oversized mountaineering sunglasses complete with leather sun-shields on the sides. The airline I waited to board was Virgin Atlantic. When I walked over to the tall window to check out the plane, my mouth fell open. The front fuselage of the jumbo jet carried the logo of a diaphanously clad female looming fifty feet tall above me. I stumbled backwards and dashed away from the gate to the nearest bar.

Pounding down a beer I suddenly caught sight of the beautiful blonde flight attendant from the Alaska flight striding by the bar in her uniform pulling a wheeled suitcase. I threw a few bills down on the bar and caught up to her.

"Oh, it's you," she said, blue eyes snapping back down the concourse.

"Hi, I didn't mean to be rude. That flight I was coming out of Alaska, the wilderness, after a long time. Michael," I said, extending my hand.

"Skyler." She shook my hand. "You look terrible. Are you OK?"

"Yeah. Just need a change of scenery. Going to London."

"London? That's where I'm going. What airline are you on?"

"Virgin."

"Oh, we both leave near the same time. Why don't you switch flights and go over with me? I'm working the flight. Won't have a lot of time to talk, but I may be able to get you into first class."

"Really?"

"Give me your ticket and I'll get you switched over."

While fortunately being served a five-course meal in first class, Skyler and I attempted to talk, but she was constantly called away by demanding passengers. We then merely nodded or smiled at one another each time she passed.

An elderly couple sat across the aisle, with their hands knitted together. I started talking with them and learned they had been married sixty-five years. I asked their secret to staying married that long.

Fred replied with a twinkle in his eyes, "Every morning when you wake up, turn to your wife, and say: 'Honey, I love you and I'm sorry,' and you have blanket coverage all day!"

I laughed, "What did you do for a living? Sell insurance?"

Fred winked. "How did you know?"

"Now you want the serious answer?" Evangeline asked.

I nodded and leaned out into the aisle.

"In all honesty, over the years there were times when we fell out of love, but then instead of giving up on each other like you young people do, we found new reasons to fall in love all over again."

Throughout the flight I kept glancing over at them, astonished at their closeness and how long they had managed to keep love alive. Fred shifted in his seat and rested his head on his wife's shoulder. While continuing to read a book, Evangeline reached up with a gnarled hand and lightly played with his hair.

The moment was so touching that I blushed and turned away from the octogenarians. *That animal show,* I thought. *Galapagos Tortoises. Live to be two hundred years old. Hit their sexual prime at eighty.*

After jotting down some talking points for the upcoming BBC interviews, I drifted off to sleep from all the champagne that Skyler had poured each time she'd walked by. Dead to the world, I slept straight through breakfast.

Near the end of the flight with the sun rising over the curvature of the earth and flooding the cabin with golden light, Skyler shook my shoulder, handed over my coat, and said, "Want to meet for a drink in London? I'm on a forty-hour layover, staying in Kensington."

"Me, too," I said, sitting up abruptly and wiping the sleep from my eyes. "How 'bout tomorrow night?"

"Great. Let's meet at a pub. The Princess Victoria at eight."

I jotted down the time and place. "Hey, Skyler."

"Hey, what?"

"Thanks for getting me on your flight and for the great meal."

Following the detailed itinerary supplied by Liz, I checked into a quaint hotel in Kensington, near Hyde Park. Approaching a hottie behind the receptionist desk, after signing in, I requested a wake-up call for mid-afternoon. She looked at me, puzzled.

"Wake-up call, you know...." I bent my head over, shut my eyes, and then pointed to my watch.

"Oh, you want me to knock you up in the afternoon?"

I nodded enthusiastically, thinking, *yes, how soon can you come!* I walked away marveling how across the pond, English can vary so much in meaning. Glancing over my shoulder again at the peaches-and-creamy clerk, I was amazed how often I fell in lust. (For some strange reason, jet-lag always made me hornier than usual—sharpened my antlers into antennae sensitive to the slightest sight of an attractive female.)

I fell asleep in the room as soon as my head hit the pillow. A knock at the door a few hours later yanked me to my feet. Having dreamed about the front desk beauty, I ran a hand through my hair and opened the door. A male bellman handed over a fax bearing the letterhead of HarperCollins, my London publisher.

> *Dear Michael: Welcome to London. I trust that everything so far has met with your approval. I will fetch you at eight a.m. prompt tomorrow for we have a full day of interviews arranged at the BBC with both the television and radio divisions. And some very good news, indeed, the BBC World News Service, going out live to two hundred countries around the globe, wants to interview you for five minutes. (They rarely interview authors. On a lark I sent a book over to them yesterday and they rang just now saying to count them in!) Please have a nice dinner and a good night's sleep. I am looking forward to being at your service all day tomorrow."*

It was signed *Jane Thomas.* I flipped through Liz's detailed itinerary and Ms. Thomas was listed as a HarperCollins handler. Already feeling horny, the job description alone felt like a physical touch. I took a cold shower, went out and wolfed down a hot meal of fish and chips at a corner stand-up, and then hit the hay early.

In bed, the front desk hottie was replaced by the *handler,* who in my imagination looked like Emma Peel from the 1960s television show *The Avengers.* She'd been a favorite of my father, who'd given me the complete megabox set of DVDs, saying, "None of the chicks today can touch Emma Peel. She was hot enough to blister paint off of walls."

I was hooked. In my raging testosterone-fueled dream, Jane Thomas was a slinky, doe-eyed spy by day and black leather-clad dominatrix by night who lashed me with a cougar-tail whip, ordered me to snog her toes, kiss her fanny, and then shag until we both howled with delight.

In the morning, showered and dressed, but still caught up in the throes of *The Avengers* dream, I glanced at my watch and looked out the window. My get-away car, a gleaming, black sedan was waiting in front of the hotel. I exited the lobby in character. Sliding into the front seat, I tipped John Steed's imaginary *bowler hat* and *brolly* to.... a short, chubby woman with chopped-off, mouse-brown hair, granny glasses, and an orange wool skirt descending down to piano-leg ankles. Jane Thomas snap-shook my hand, then stomped on the gas.

Inside the BBC edifice, they signed us in at a big desk and we were whisked into studio after studio for brief radio and TV interviews. I was surprised at the BBC's antiquated equipment. With the rest of the world rapidly going digital, the microphones were old, bulky, steel-perforated stand-ups. The hosts were named Nigel or Colin, with dandruff on the shoulders of their cardigan sweaters and, seated they curled thin, bandy legs over and around their thighs instead of the macho American way of resting ankle-on-knee (not wanting to pinch the package).

I was introduced to Shawn Mahoney for a *Down-the-Line* interview, broadcast simultaneously throughout England, Ireland, Scotland, and Wales. As we settled into our studio seats, off-mike, Mahoney chortled, "Laddie, yu muust come to Irelan fur thee bess luukin' wymen on Gud's faire earthe!" Then live at the top of the interview after a snappy introduction, Mahoney hit me with, "Wale, Mister Bachler of The Yeer, wot du yu luk fur furst in a gurl—luuks or personality? Be hunast, mahn!"

Expecting to talk about my Alaska book, I was caught off guard, but quickly shifted gears. "Of course, I'm attracted to beauty, who isn't? But I want a woman who has depth; who I can talk to for hours at a time about everything under the sun. When a woman lights me up mentally that can be as exciting as physically, sometimes even more so."

After the interview a female BBC producer came on in my headphones saying in a clipped, melodic, British accent, "Mikal, thot was absolute-lee *SMASHING!*"

Before I could even say thanks, Jane tore off my headphones and yanked me by the arm for a full-tilt rush into a tiny elevator and a slow, herky-jerky ascension up into the dark, padded soundproof womb of the BBC WORLD NEWS SERVICE. Seeing the words in big block letters on the entrance wall, I gulped, remembering how my grandfather listened to this program every night in New York City, fine-tuning his shortwave radio, then hanging on every crisply delivered word.

The current host, Millicent Myers, had me sign her copy of *Inside Passage*, my Alaskan adventure book. A producer outside a glass panel held up a hand, fingers spread wide. He then dropped each digit in rapid succession. Down to one—he pointed directly at Millicent. A red light flashed on and we were locked, just the two of us, in a tiny booth with people listening in two hundred countries around the world.

Millicent was so full of praise for my writing that I couldn't believe my ears. She started out by saying that I was responsible for her sleepless night last evening and *not* because I was the *Cosmopolitan* Bachelor.... *Smooth,* I thought. She went on about how she started *Inside Passage* and read it all the way through until the sun came up—she was that captivated. Her questions were exactly what I wanted to be asked—inquiries about Alaska's whales, glaciers, northern lights, and magical mysticism.

Millicent Myers wrapped up the interview saying, "and this young man, a rare combination of action and reflection, courage and sensitivity is, mark my words, soon to be famous around the world."

After thanking her over and over, I floated out of the booth in a daze.

Then as quickly as the string of interviews started, we were finished. Handler Jane sped me off to the hotel, but I was too wound up post-performances to be held captive by the small, drab room. In the lobby, I turned up my wool pea coat collar against a chill wind and charged out into London, filled with wonder and disbelief. *Was I really on the fabled BBC? And The World News Service, no less!*

I stopped across the street from Harrods Department Store, watching a white limo halt in front of the palatial edifice, the temple of luxury retail. The driver opened two doors and an endless stream of women in black burqas hopped out onto the sidewalk. The only thing showing was their flashing eyes. Even though it was a stretch limo an inordinate number of women poured forth, finally followed by a short, roly-poly sheik. The women stood momentarily at attention, the sheik raised his palms, and they dove through the revolving doors into Harrods.

*Animal show,* I thought: *Bull walrus with his harem. One female is too many—a dozen, not enough.*

As I turned away and entered Hyde Park, a beautiful woman in a silver-metallic coat strode toward me, her long black hair swishing over the shiny fabric. Wanting to try out my new favorite adjective, I murmured, "Smashing," as she passed. Over her shoulder, she shot me a dazzling smile and a blue-eyed glow that scorched my heart.

Nervous energy expended and now exhausted from the day, I wandered aimlessly through Kensington. The night turned bitter cold. I glanced at my watch. *Twenty minutes till Skyler.* Looking up, there across the street was the pub…our meeting place.

The Princess Victoria gleamed kelly green and looked so inviting with the large center window bathed in flickering orange reflections from a fireplace. The place was packed; loud talk and laughter spilled out onto the street as I tugged open the door. I scanned the bar and tables for Skyler. *Not here.* So as not to miss her when she came in, I made myself conspicuous at the end of the long mahogany bar.

No sooner did I order a pint of beer than the fairytale *Goldilocks* herself was standing before me. A stunning sylph of a girl under a tumbling cascade of golden curls.

"I saw you on the telly. On the Beeb you were, weren't you?" She leaned in closer. "YES! 'Tis you—the bachelor bloke who lived with the whales!"

I dropped my head, embarrassed.

"Gwendolyn," she said, her small hand fluttering toward me like a sparrow's wing.

"Bond, James Bond."

Gwendolyn giggled as if no female had ever giggled before, a series of squeaky bubbles of enchantment that popped alluringly against my ears. "No, you're not!"

"I know, just always wanted to say that someday in London to a beautiful girl." I blinked a few times, trying to reboot—not quite believing that this exquisite, ethereal creature was real, let alone standing before me.

Her hand rested on my arm. "Can I ask a favor?"

Aroused by her touch, I would do anything for this paragon of purity: slay fire-breathing dragons, take on entire armies, endure all twelve of Hercules' labors—*Hell, add one more!*—absolutely anything to please M'lady, Princess Gwendolyn. "Sure!"

"My boyfriend saw you on the telly, too...." she pointed to a leather-jacketed giant with a Mohawk haircut died chartreuse and a face that could split wood, "…we haven't been getting along," Gwendolyn cooed mournfully. "If you pretend you fancy me maybe he'll get jealous and…"

The last thing I saw was Skyler walk through the door…stop…turn and dash off as a fist crashed into my face. The world went black.

The barkeep was shaking me. I awoke on the floor of the pub, flat on my back, feeling as if my head was busted in half. The crowd was gone. A hefty woman hauled me to my feet and handed over ice wrapped in a towel. "Never saw it comin' didja?"

I shook my head, then felt like vomiting.

"Ralphus charged over here like Ragin' Bull, himself," the barkeep said. "Hit ya with a right cross, then a left uppercut. Fan of the fights, I am, but not in my pub. No sir! Yur gunna have quite a shiner 'rund that eye once tha swellin' gous down. Luky he dint break yur beek."

I mumbled thanks and pointed to the towel. The barkeep nodded and opened the door. I staggered out into the frigid night, massive ice pack pressed against a throbbing eye.

"Smashing...." I cursed.

On the flight home to New York as I continued to ice my eye in an aisle seat, a portly, middle-aged man in amenity kit slippers shuffled unhurriedly down the aisle from the restroom and stopped next to me. "Christ, kid, looks like you went twelve rounds with Mike Tyson."

"Jealous boyfriend."

"Give as good as you got?"

I shook my head slowly. "Never saw it coming."

The man winced. "Hey, you look familiar.... I know, you're that *Cosmo* guy! My office is in Times Square. I see your billboard picture every day out my window. Well, I'll be damned," he said.

"Aren't you in the papers a lot," I asked, "society page, your picture with different women?"

"Yeah, we're sort of in the same business…only I try not to get beat up. Joey Famina," he said, extending his hand.

I shook and said, "What's that word they use to describe you?"

"A walker."

"What does that mean exactly? I've always wondered."

"Well, I escort women to social events: the opera, symphony, and parties if their husbands are out of town or not interested in going."

"How do you meet them all?"

"Among the wealthy, New York is a small town. One tells a friend and she tells a friend and…"

"So on. Do the husbands ever get jealous?"

"From the looks of me, you can tell I'm no threat. I'm toad-ugly and I know it; however..." Famina leaned over, "it's really my cover. Give me ten minutes talking with a woman and I erase my face."

"Never heard it put that way before."

"Well," he said, peering closer at my battered eye and cheek, "you might have to do some temporary *face erasing* of your own. Men are seduced through the eyes, women through their ears and their noses. Remember that, kid, and you'll go far."

"Thanks. Good to meet you," I said, shaking his hand again.

Famina patted my shoulder. "Be careful out there."

Returning to my apartment building, I stabbed a key into my mailbox, one tarnished brass square amidst many in the antiquated lobby. The leaden door popped open and a torrent of letters poured down onto the floor. The elevator that hardly ever worked opened and an elegant, elderly woman stepped out.

"Hello, Mrs. Auchingloss," I said as I attempted to gather up the envelopes.

The woman stepped gingerly around the puddles of mail, sniffing the air. "I managed the perfume department at Bloomingdale's for thirty-four years. My, my...." She sniffed some more. "There's quite a skirmish going on here. *Obsession* is clashing with *Musc Ravageur*, with *Shalimar* on the sidelines."

As I stood up with the mail clutched against my chest, she slowly looked me up and down. "Whatever you have...*that* should be bottled!" She glanced at my swollen black eye. "A fighter *and* a lover. No wonder you're catnip to the ladies." Mrs. Auchingloss winked, then broke into a coltish two-step dance on her way out the door.

I shook my head and bolted up the stairs. The phone was ringing as I opened the apartment door. Hearing Liz on the answering machine, I picked up.

"Hi, darlin'...how did London go?"

"Smashing. I even got on the BBC World News Service."

"I heard, Michael, that's wonderful! They *never* feature first-time authors and hardly any authors at all. Harper-UK really came through."

"Yes, they did. I thanked them in an e-mail from the airport. And thank you, Liz, for getting it off the ground."

"I love London. Always max out my credit cards at Harrods. Did you have any time to enjoy yourself?"

"Um, well—I got into a bar fight and now have a black eye."

"You didn't."

"I did, but I didn't do anything. Long story."

"Let me guess. There was a woman involved?"

"Yep."

"Was the press there?"

"No, after hours."

"Thank, God. Well, heal up fast. I'm getting a lot of requests for you. Hey, I have a favor to ask," she continued. "I also represent Howard Stern and it seems he heard about your little Halloween soirée and was very impressed. He wants you on his shows, both radio and the TV-thing on *E*."

I thought about it for a moment then said, "That's not the image I want to project."

"Oh, and a hundred hookers all shouting your name in the streets *is?*"

"They weren't hookers and I had nothing to do with it."

"Work with me here. I can't turn Howard down. Please reconsider."

"Liz, it's getting totally out of control. I want to pull back a bit. How about this. Instead of me, how about a TA?"

"Tits and Ass?"

"No, teaching assistant. Three guys from Rathbone's Science Department are screening all the *Cosmo* mail and stuff. They've seen far more than me."

"I doubt if Howard will go for just that."

"Well, then—how about one of the girls I dated?"

"Now you're talking. Makes you look even better, being aloof, mysterious. Have one of the girls talk about you. Keeps you in a no-fly zone and kinda nudges you toward *Legend* territory. Tell me about her."

"She's a body double in Hollywood, has the *Best Butt in the Business.* I met her in San Francisco after the book signing. We were walking up one of the hills to a B&B and a guy fell off a cable car looking at her and two cars crashed. She said she accentuates her asset by doing what Marilyn Monroe did—shaves an eighth-of-an-inch off the bottom of her right high heel."

"BINGO! Howard will love her. An eighth-of-an-inch, huh? I'll have to send all my Jimmy Choos out to a carpenter."

"Shareen used to be a wood-worker." I paused, remembering her in bed. "She still is," I muttered.

"What?"

"I mean, she…she can shave your shoes."

"Have her call me."

"Yes, ma'am."

# 11

## "...a Tornado in a Teacup"

As Ellen opened her door, she shrieked upon seeing my purple and saffron-ringed eye.

"*Ah cudda bin a contendah,*" I said, shuffling into the penthouse.

"Morani, you look terrible! What happened to you?"

After I explained, she announced: "Raw meat."

"What?"

"You need raw meat to draw out the swelling and calm down that bruise. Like fighters do."

"You mean that's for real, not just for effect like in the movies?"

"Steak tartare will work. It's Jeeves night off...I'll see if we have any." She strode off to the kitchen and returned shortly. "No. All out. Wait a minute...." she said, a wicked grin spreading across her face, "I have something that will work even better." In two smooth moves, Ellen pulled her sweater over her head and reached back to unhook her bra. She stood topless before me.

"*Whoa! S*ex cures a black eye? Hey, slow down; I need a little romance here."

"Oh, Morani, you're such a wimp. Lie back on the love seat and shut your eye...and your mouth."

I did as told.

Ellen stood at the head of the narrow settee and leaned over me, cupping her right breast in her hand and placing it carefully against my right eye socket. Her nipple slid into the corner of my eye and the sleek, cool curve of her breast pressed down against the throbbing ache, drawing out the pain.

"Umm.... Ellen?"

"Yeah?"

"I think Goldilocks' bear tagged my left eye as well."

"Greedy, greedy." She palmed her left breast into place, as well.

"Know what?" I murmured.

"What?"

"I can see God."

"Sure it's not the devil?" she said, her hand snaking southward to unzip my pants.

Afterward, with Ellen in the bathroom, I lay there in a relaxed daze. My eye no longer hurt. I shook my head and smiled. *Amazing, everything this woman knows.*

Ellen returned, still naked, and sat back smugly, legs curled under her in a black leather chair.

*Animal show,* I thought again. *Panther. Unpredictable. Exciting. Man-eater twitching her tail.* I stared at her. "It's amazing how comfortable you are in your skin. You're not like any woman I've ever met."

Ellen lit a cigarillo, then pursed her lips and puffed out two tight smoke rings. "I like to shake things up. Like I told you before, my idea of Hell is when sex becomes routine or predictable. That's why we should never get married and always be free to have other lovers."

Her statement hit me like dry ice. "What about jealousy? Wouldn't you be jealous if you knew I was with other women?"

"HELLO. Earth to Morani! You *are* with other women, Mr. *Cosmo* Bachelor, and have I gotten upset? In fact, I ask about your other girls."

"True, but not even a whit or pang of jealousy?"

"*Whit* or *pang?* Sounds like somebody just got back from England. No, jealousy stems from insecurity and the selfish need to own or possess someone. As the saying goes: 'You don't truly have something until you set it free.' You are very much your totem animal, Morani. An eagle dies if kept in a cage. Your nature is to be wild and free."

"True."

"But you're not that different than most men. Men and many women crave variety and excitement." She paused to blow smoke. "You said before that I shock you; I turn you on with how different I am."

I nodded.

"It's because I'm sick and tired of the slut double standard where women have to repress our sexuality and men don't. When Kinsey did his study on sex and wrote *Sexual Behavior in the Human Male* it was a raging bestseller. When he published *Sexual Behavior in the Human Female* it tanked. Everyone was appalled… no one believed females really acted like that."

She rolled her eyes. "We have the same double standard decades later. The sex drive in women is as strong—or stronger—than men's. It's time now for us to have our jollies. GAWD! Your British vernacular is contagious." She flicked an ash. "Besides, marriage is where a man's penis goes to die."

"Whoa. That's extreme."

"It's true. A few months ago, I gave a lecture on the Northwest Coast Natives… your people in Alaska. During the talk, I showed a slide of the totem pole *The Woman Who Married a Bear.* Afterwards a woman came up to me with her husband in tow. She said: 'All women marry bears. Our job is to tame them!' And she said it with such slam-the-door satisfaction in front of her slumped-over husband he might as well have had an iron collar around his neck attached to a chain."

"Marriage castrates a man," Ellen continued authoritatively. "Denying a man his very nature, insisting that he settle down with her and her only, a wife turns a man into a steer. No wonder when married, put out to pasture, a man's vitality and virility dry up."

"It's the *Coolidge Effect,*" I told her.

"The what?"

"I once read that when President Coolidge and his wife were separately touring a chicken farm the guide told Mrs. Coolidge that the rooster mated a dozen times a day. 'Tell that to Mr. Coolidge!' the Mrs. said."

"When Mr. Coolidge went on his tour, the guide informed him that the rooster mated a dozen times a day. Coolidge asked, 'With the same hen?' The guide replied, 'No…with twelve different hens.' The President replied, 'Tell that to Mrs. Coolidge!' "

"Precisely my point. We don't eat the same meal, wear the same shirt or dress day after day. To stimulate muscle growth at the gym it's best to vary the routine every six weeks or the body stagnates—the same exercise that once was effective no longer works. Our hair gets overly accustomed to one shampoo, the shaft gets coated. You don't read just one book over and over all your life. You want to read many books, learn new things."

I nodded and stood up. I walked over to a bowl of nuts on a side table. I tossed one into my mouth. "I love nuts. They're good for you. Used to buy walnuts all the time, then just almonds…then didn't like either anymore. My favorite is these," I lifted up a handful, "mixed nuts…you get an assortment of different flavors."

I walked back to the love seat and sat down. "When we—our generation looks at our parents, it's scary. Marriage rarely seems to work. Divorce after divorce. Everyone is just hooking up now…putting off commitment."

"Want to know why?" she asked.

"Yes."

"The answer is in your hand."

I stared at the nuts. "You mean the variety?"

Ellen nodded. "It's that simple. Marriage isn't natural and what isn't natural doesn't last. Less than three percent of the animal kingdom is monogamous. And in one thousand out of eleven hundred and fifty-four human societies, past and present, polygamy prevails. It's why our culture is so fucked up. Monogamous marriage and religious repression may very well cause the sinking depression and epidemic ingesting of antidepressants in the richest have-it-all nation on earth. As Freud said: 'Happiness is sexual happiness.' "

"Freud also said: 'Sometimes a cigar is just a cigar.' "

Ellen waved her cigarillo around the room at the tribal art. "Other cultures far older, wiser, and more sophisticated than ours know that sex is a sacred, creative force having nothing to do with sin. Even religion and art are sublimations of the sex drive. No matter how we try, the sex drive will not fit into the confines of institutional or moralistic boxes. It's like trying to catch a tornado in a teacup."

"Speaking of tea, could we make some?"

"Sure. Good idea." She stubbed out the cigarillo. "You stay. I'll make it."

Ellen returned still naked and holding two cups of steaming lapsang souchong tea.

I tasted. "Umm…delicious, thank you."

As we sipped, I said, "You know, I'm confused about what exactly constitutes cheating. Is talking in-depth with another woman, not your wife or committed partner, cheating on them? I mean you can get more intimate talking for far longer and deeper than you can fuck. Well, maybe excluding *you*."

She smiled.

"And I just read today in *The Post* where a guy's wife filed for divorce after she discovered he had a girlfriend in *Second Life*, the online virtual world."

"Yeah, and did you see real lifeguy's picture? He weighs like three hundred pounds and his online avatar was *Rip Studly*."

"Wonder if the divorce will hold up in court? Is it technically adultery if the other person doesn't have a heartbeat?"

"Don't know. Hmm…does a battery-powered paramour count? Most of my women friends have vibrators that they use when their husbands or boyfriends or both are out of town or not around. They even have names for their vibes."

"What? I thought naming your Johnson came solely under male jurisdiction. What do they call them?"

"Jack Rabbit. Steely Dan. Hello Kitty. Did you know the rock band Steely Dan took its name from a dildo in a William Burroughs novel?"

"Didn't know that."

"And just wait," Ellen said, setting her teacup down. "The floodgates are going to open in the virtual direction. I have a friend in Japan, brilliant guy I went to school with, who is into A.I.—artificial intelligence and bio-robotics. He said it's an all-out race right now to see who finalizes and locks in the patent on female robots with human-like limbs and flexible polymers as artificial skin. He says that fully-functional fem-bots are maybe two generations away, middle of this century. Can you imagine? Marriage will be obsolete if men can have a different woman every night with interchangeable parts."

A similar sentiment echoed in my head from Ralph, the TA: *"There are very few women I want to spend my life with, but thousands I want to spend a night with."*

"I've been thinking lately how amazing female anatomy is. Like most men, I'm *cunt-struck*—totally obsessed."

"How so?"

"Imagine asking an engineer to design something that looks like a flower and has the feel of the softest velvet and implant it on and in a female human being. From behind, it's positioned beneath a breathtakingly curved split-globe that itself is as smooth as silk, or from the front you are guided to *la flora* by two upswept pillars, shapely legs… highways to heaven. The flower itself is bright pink, becomes engorged and shiny when excited, and as it moistens with nectar it warms at the same time and clutches a finger, tongue or penis tight as a fist—yet can expand big enough to birth a baby. And, oh yeah, if stimulated in a proper manner, it snaps and flutters in a series of orgasms, giving off a scent like heavenly ambrosia and tastes like Mango Tanqueray. Is it any wonder why men are addicted and obsessed?"

"Picasso said a woman's genitalia looks like an exclamation mark, asshole included," Ellen said.

"But the trouble is women are the strict gatekeepers of said object of obsession and allow male access sparingly."

"Ha! Not you. Not now. You're in up to your ears," she laughed.

"Yeah, but for most guys and for me before my fifteen minutes of fame, the female flower is hard to pollinate. There's that saying: *The trouble is women have all the pussy.*"

"Even in prison," she said. "Did you know that sometimes when a guy is butt-fucking another guy, so as not to be thought of as gay, the fucker unfolds on the back of the fuckee a naked centerfold woman from a wank-mag, with her legs spread apart just above the butthole of Ben Dover?"

"Uhhh...." I didn't know what to say.

"The Power *is* in the pussy. Women know it and convicts, too," she explained.

"Hope I never get arrested."

"The truth is," Ellen continued, "we are polyamorous beings living in a repressed, puritanical world. Monogamy is so oppressive. It's time for a change."

She leaned forward. "Studies show that when a man is away from his wife, his testosterone level and sperm count jump. Women are much more likely to orgasm and be impregnated during coitus with a lover than with their husbands. That the cure for impotence isn't these stupid boner drugs with awful side effects, but simply the injection of a fresh partner. This may not be how society wants it, but that's how it *is.* Like a stream paved over, tidy concrete may cover it, but the natural force rages on."

"Biology is destiny," I commented.

"Yes, it's not a *sin*...it's science. And in many ways it isn't even subliminal. We're directed by our genitals. Being infolded, women are far more self-involved than men. We think the world revolves around us," she said.

I nodded. "One time I walked into a party and saw a guy with the same dress shirt on. We grinned and said, 'Great taste, man.' Another party, two women arrived in the same dress. Both threw down a hissy-fit."

"It's because biologically, women *are* wrapped up in themselves," she said. "A guy cheats on a woman simply because he wants a piece of strange for a change, a bowl of spicy pasta instead of the same old salmon. We fly into a rage because he cheated on *ME!* No, he didn't. He's only being a man, doing what he is programmed by nature and millions of years of evolution to do. Every morning when a man wakes up his testicles have produced millions of new sperm—baby-batter waiting to be flung far and wide. One teenage boy has enough sperm in a single ejaculate to populate the entire planet. Women are so wrapped up in ourselves because our cunts, literally, are folded flowers—whereas for men sex is mostly external, out there away from the center of you."

"So that's why women like flowers so much."

"Yeah, they remind us of ourselves. In nature, flowers are the sex organs of plants. No different with us. Look at a drawing of a woman's reproductive system. It's very much like an orchid."

"All valid points," I said, pausing to sip my tea, "but you're leaving out one very important thing."

"What's that?"

"Love."

"Ah, love...." Ellen set down her tea cup, "as Tina Turner sings: *What's love got to do with it?* It's animal attraction not love that creates the urge to merge. Love is artificial, man-made B.S. The sappy side of lust. You think you have love locked up, wrapped in cozy ribbons, and then one day you don't have it at all. Where did it go? Thin air, because that's what it was made of to begin with. Lust lasts. Love is the mind's way of making sex, the wild thang, acceptable. Women twist lust into love so they aren't sluts and to convince themselves the horny guy who just wants to fuck them is *Mr. Right* or, up violins…her *Soulmate.* Bullshit! Love is nothing more than a chemical reaction, a revved-up eruption of dopamine: a natural amphetamine. And in each case, that euphoria's got an expiration date, programmed to last two, three years tops, and then it drops off…big time. It's purely a biological reaction. Nature's way to propagate the species. Simple as that: chemical fact instead of hearts-and-flowers fiction."

"Awfully cold and clinical, Ms. Klein."

"No, just rock-bottom realistic."

"If that's the case, why do we do this to ourselves? Why do we set such impossible, unnatural standards that cause such madness and misery?"

Ellen got up and moved around the room. In the semi-darkness she *was* a panther, the way she padded around—her tail twitching in time with a fully engaged mind.

"Romantic love was invented by the troubadours in the fifteenth century, the cheesy Hallmark card artists of their day." She paused to stand directly in front of me. "You know how most holidays—Mother's Day, Valentine's Day, even Christmas just exist to stimulate the economy, get people to buy shit they don't need, or flood restaurants with mothers? This romantic love stuff has created the biggest industry of them all. If we finally stopped buying this sappy, pie-in-the-sky crap, entire economies would collapse, with florists, bakeries, wedding planners, greeting card companies, and half of all photographers and third-rate musicians shutting up shop, to say nothing of doctors, psychiatrists, jewelers, and divorce lawyers that would no longer be needed."

"The other night I rented *The African Queen.*"

"Great flick," she said, reaching across me to the table to grab a few nuts.

"One line had me wondering—when Katherine Hepburn's character says: 'Nature, Mr. Allnut, is what we are put in this world to rise above.' "

"Yeah," Ellen said, "and risk losing our connection to reality itself and the wellspring of vitality and joy! I believe in what nature and evolution have created, not what man in the name of religion has decreed and foisted upon us."

She walked along the wall of primitive art, eating. "What if we got it wrong all along? What if we know next to nothing about the true purpose of sex? What if in the past two thousand years our culture has been totally deceived by warped priests, led away from our true nature?"

She padded back over to me and in one smooth move sat in my lap. "There is an exception. Anselm Grün, a very courageous monk, once wrote that when we reach down into our passions we find that they lead us directly up to God."

Later that night, back in my apartment, exhausted I wrote:

*THEOREM #4: ALPHA FEMALE*

Ellen Klein is breaking new ground and her beliefs may be where men and women will evolve—in five hundred years, if we ever summon enough honesty and courage to *get real* with one another and see the true nature of sex and proceed from there. E.K. sees The Big Picture as a cultural anthropologist, synthesizing many perspectives on men and women and uses Nature as the working template. First and foremost we are animals (just dress it up a little), biology is destiny, and we would be much happier if we accept and embrace our animal natures instead of trying to pretend we have surpassed or are *better* than the instinctual operating system.

And on a personal level, Ellen is perfect for me. By allowing me my freedom to see other women—it only makes me want her more.

# 12

# Chama

**Vivi Correa**

**Species Name:** *Goddess Tropicali Sambatastic*
**Habitat & Range:** Jungles and beaches of Brazil.
**Identifying Characteristics:** Dazzling, primary-colored plumage in constant hypnotic motion.
**Also called:** The Bird of Paradise.
**Best Known For:** Instantly instilling in males Amour Fu (Crazy Love).

As I was finishing breakfast in my apartment, Charlie snoozed, purring up a rhythmic rattle in my lap. The phone rang. I set Charlie down, still asleep, on the couch and answered. It was Liz checking on how my research was progressing.

"I don't know," I said. Instead of telling her about Ellen I decided to hold back. "If women confounded Freud, what chance do I have at figuring them out?"

"Well, from what Shareen said on Howard Stern's show, you're man enough for the job. Did you see it?"

"No," I cringed. "What happened?"

"It was only his highest-rated show ever," she chortled.

"You're kidding?"

"No. She had Howard eating out of her hand when she walked in wearing nothing but a tool belt. And guess what else?"

"What?"

"She left International Creative Management for lil' ole me."

I shook my head, smiling, remembering our time together.

"But I have my work cut out for me. Shareen said she's tired of being a sex object. She really wants to direct."

"Oh. Well, she's been on enough movie sets to have learned the craft, I guess."

"Hey, not to change the subject—and don't be mad my dear, but I volunteered you as the main event, the grand finale for this year's United Way *Bid-for-Bachelors* auction. It's a good cause. A benefit for United Way and a nice bit of pub for you and the book since the affair is televised, but first go to Armani and get a custom-fitted tux. You can afford it. Disney just optioned your book."

"Wow. Liz, that's great! Thank you for Disney. Great work." I then furrowed my brow. "But that other thing—the Bid for Bachelors. You want me to parade in front of hundreds of women like a piece of meat, and on television? NO WAY!"

"Michael, you have to maximize your fifteen minutes of fame. Most authors would kill for this kind of publicity. It's not enough anymore to just write in some garret or on a remote island. Writers today have to get out there and push the product or they don't remain published authors for very long."

I gave a long drawn-out sigh. "Liz, can I ask you something?"

"Shoot darlin'."

"Would my book have gotten published if I was ugly?"

"Want an honest answer?"

"Yes."

"Probably not. Unfortunately, TV is the medium that sells books today and if a first-time author isn't telegenic it's double-tough to break into the biz. We have a saying in Texas: *If it ain't pretty, don't put it out on the front porch.* Shouldn't be that way but the cold, hard truth is that, pardon the cliché, sex sells. Too bad it's the *sizzle* that's made such a big deal of and not the steak itself. But if the sizzle gets them to take a bite of the meat, well that's the way the cookie crumbles. Hey, how's that for mixing metaphors?"

"I'll think about it. But, if I do agree to do it, it's crazy to spend all that money for the one-time use of a tux. I'll just rent."

"You'll be needing it again, probably soon—for your wedding. You don't want to be *all hat and no ranch*, as Daddy used to say."

"No way. I'm never getting married. I'm having way too much fun playing the field."

Liz was silent for a moment. "Michael, are you really having fun?"

"Yeah, I really am," I said.

"We'll see. I have a bet with Rathbone that some girl you've either met already or a new filly in tomorrow's mail is going to wrap you around her little finger."

"Liz, I have a confession to make."

"Oh, God. What? No, don't tell me. . .you already have a wife up in Alaska. Some native woman that you've already rubbed more than noses with."

"I'm gay."

"Oh, stop. If you're gay, then Howdy Doody ain't made of wood."

After hanging up the phone, I felt the need for company. I decided to check in with Mission Control. Twenty minutes later, I walked through Rathbone's front door, then stopped abruptly. The room, always so neatly organized, as tight as a ship, now looked as if a big storm had hit. Letters and lingerie were scattered all over the floor; the once pinned-up pictures had fallen or been pulled down from the walls and each of the TAs were standing there dumb-struck and wearing bright crimson lipstick kisses on their cheeks.

"What happened? Looks like a bomb went off in here."

"It just did!" Steve said, wide-eyed.

"Vivi Correa. . ." Kwame mumbled.

"Who? What?" I said.

Ralph stepped forward, grinning. "Just a few friendly kisses thrown around. That's all."

"We were going to call you," Steve added. "But it happened so fast we didn't have time to pick up the phone."

"Will someone please explain what the…"

"From what we gathered," Ralph interrupted, "she's a dancer with *Brazil! Brazil!!* It's a tour group performing over at The Apollo. He pointed to an ad in the paper.

Here," he handed it to me, "seems she saw you in *Cosmo* and on the billboard in Times Square. She's coming to your crib later tonight after their final performance."

"WHAT! You gave out my home address?"

"Don't be mad. Believe me, you'll thank us later," Steve grinned from ear to ear.

My anger defused as I scanned their awed and beaming faces. "Viva what?"

"VIVI CORREA!" they all chorused.

"Did she leave a note or a phone number?"

They shook their heads.

"Doesn't speak English, but, bro…she doesn't need to," Kwame said dreamily.

"What time?"

"She didn't say," Ralph responded.

"All she kept saying was—here, I wrote it down: *Moço da natureza.* It's Spanish, I think," Steve said.

"No, it would be Portuguese since she's from Brazil," Ralph added. "I can find out what she said. . ." He grabbed the scrap of paper from Steve and sat down at the computer, jumping on a Foreign Language/English translation website. "Nature Boy," Ralph tapped the screen. "That's what she was saying."

"No doubt now about what she wants!" Kwame smiled.

"Clear your calendar, take a nap, and you better pull a *Rocky*—drink some raw eggs for energy," Steve advised.

I blushed as I turned to leave. *I'll never get used to this.* I stopped at The Gotham Book Mart on my way home to pick up an English/Portuguese dictionary.

That evening, I waited and waited, then waited some more. Flashing back over the state of the disheveled Mission Control and my dazed buddies, my pulse pounded and I couldn't concentrate on writing or reading. I flipped through the Portuguese dictionary trying to memorize a few basic words, but the simple salutations quickly faded away. Nothing stuck in such restless suspense. I paced around the room, trying to release pent-up energy and lower my heart rate. Finally, from nervous exhaustion, I stretched out across the bed. I was fast asleep when the security buzzer rang.

"Yes?" I said groggily at the intercom box, glancing at the clock. It was just past midnight.

*"Moça da natureza?"*

With a trembling hand, I pressed the button to unlock the outer door. I ran to the window. A large white van pulled away. I opened my apartment door and sat back on the couch, waiting forever for her to appear.

She entered through the doorway bowing, one hand holding a tall headdress in place, the other suppressing something large behind her. Once inside the doorway she stood up and let go. Like a peacock on display, gold and fuchsia-colored feathers sprang out around her. She was topped by a crown covered with sequins in the shape of fiery suns. Her brown breasts were mostly bare. She was a feathered angel, a sultry temptress, a bird of paradise, a solar flare.

"Oi, me chamo Vivi!" she said with a smile that jumped from her lips to her eyes.

"Oi, me chamo Michael," I replied.

Her eyes sparkled when she asked, "Você fala português?"

To be sure of what I was hearing, I picked up the dictionary and paged frantically through it: *você* (you) and *fala* (speak). I shrugged, holding up the book.

From deep in the feathers she extracted a silver disc and held it out to me. Coming from such an other-worldly being, at first I was taken aback. Then seeing that the disc had a hole in the middle, recognition kicked-in. I put the CD in my player and following her lead pushed back some of the furniture. She pointed at me then the couch. I sat down.

Looking with disbelief at this dazzling creature in my own living room, no less, my eyes were then filled with wonder and my ears with awe as drums flooded the room, Pulsating layers of rhythm from wildest Brazil and Africa, rooted deep in Vivi Correa's DNA that lifted her feet and swung her hips in a two-step samba rhythm, flinging me into a *fantasia*. Watching her dance, unfurling her native life and history before me, I was no longer in gritty New York City, but transported far away on a feathered cloud, soaring over lush green jungle and a tri-colored sea.

The drumming increased and with her back to me, she unhinged, unhooked and dropped her costume. Wearing just a white feathery thong, her dark body shook and shimmered up and down. Then a subversive high-pitched drum cut in. The squeaky, irregular rhythms caused her bare left hip to quiver and lift and somehow jump from side to side while the other hip remained still.

The river of drums flooded back as a righteous force, admonishing, drowning the *cuíca*, but moments later it rose again in rebellion and she reveled in its essence. Cosmic Eros that she shunted back and forth from heaven to earth with both hips that even now though she stood statue-still seemed to buck around the room, pulling in, jumping out, then collapsing back into themselves and shaking together with a final quivering spasm—the very movements that created the universe.

The music stopped, but my heart continued to boom. Vivi turned around, sweat coating her skin with a brilliant sheen. I picked up the dictionary and barked: "Inacreditável!" (Incredible.)..."Obrigado!" (Thank you.) I blurted: "Quente!" (Hot.) And long moments later, fumbling, finally found, "Muito." (Very). I flung the book down.

I was out-of-my-head drunk with lust, love, fierce longing for this woman. I would give her anything—money, blood, a house, my unborn children, a Lamborghini. I would rob and kill for her.

I remembered the bottle of Cristal Champagne I had stashed in the bottom of the refrigerator for a special occasion. I popped the cork and hurriedly looked for glasses. They were all dirty in the sink. I rushed back throwing myself on the couch. *We don't need no stinkin' glasses.*

Vivi sauntered over to the couch. Her taut curves unfurling now in slow motion were stunning. With a circular twist she sat down next to me. Close up her beauty was even more breathtaking. Her lips were full and carmine red. She had large onyx eyes, mocha skin so smooth it looked poreless. I stared mesmerized and open-mouthed. As she reached for the champagne bottle, a pert, black nipple grazed my arm. I gulped. Now I knew she was real. *What did I ever do to be worthy of this?*

We each drank from the bottle passing it back and forth without taking our eyes from each other's. The entire dictionary, English and Portuguese, was spoken in our locked gaze. Then Vivi stood up and in a fluid motion unsnapped the last bit of costume framing her hips. I leapt up and my clothes flew away as if on wires.

Before getting into bed, she made the sign of the cross. Naked now together on our sides, Vivi ran her hand over my ass. Her extravagant red lips expanded into a luscious grin as she made a flat motion with her hand. She then pushed me over on my back, slithered on top and placed my hands on her hips.

"Bum bum," she said.

I lifted my hands from the *requintada* (exquisite) mounds and made abrupt half-circle curves in the air. She laughed, then nuzzled and sniffed my neck. I looked down over her mocha-brown back and legs, contrasted so beautifully, deliciously against the white sheets. I reached into the nightstand, tore open a condom packet with my teeth, and put it on.

She lifted her head and brushed her mouth over mine. Her tongue flicked out at the corners and then slid in dead center, as sweet as candy. She sucked my bottom lip as she opened her legs on top of me. I gasped. I had never felt such heat before.

"*Chama,*" she purred, understanding perfectly, as her eyes smiled and danced and rolled back with delight.

Guided by her rhythmic motions, I soared into and through places I had never been before. I opened my eyes often to see for certain that there was a woman in my bed and not a goddess bearing erotic gifts. Music flowed from our embraces. I felt silk, smelled cocoa, tasted mango and pungent papaya, and in my fortunate ear—heard a *tigressa* howl.

A lifetime later, I was lifted from satiation, from deep slumber by the rustling of wings. Vivi was getting dressed. I sat up. She turned with a sad face and pointed to the clock. She threw her arms around me. We fell back on the bed and ravished each other once more before she flew away.

When I awakened hours later, I felt reborn. *Had to be a dream—a double-feature…….* As I rolled over, something tickled my ass. I reached down and plucked up a fuchsia-colored feather. I stayed in bed most of the day, feather over my heart, drugged on bliss.

Hands crossed behind my head, flat on my back, in my mind I played over and over again in the slowest, sweetest motion each and every moment with Vivi. At one point, I hit the memory pause button, got up, and returned to bed with the dictionary. The very page I opened to showed the word I sought: *chama*. It meant flame.

Finally, I got up and went into the living room sticking the fuchsia feather in my hair. Something else confirmed she had really been there. Under the half-full bottle of Cristal was a note in a feminine hand.

> *Te espero no Rio, vou te levar para o Pão de Açúcar e te levar a loucura nos braços de Iemanjá nas nossas praias e vamos dançar ao som de Tom Jobim na Floresta da Tijuca! Os Americanos tem medo do prazer. Prazer produz energia e felicidade. Mas você e diferente gato, tem a alma Brasileira!"*

Her name and phone number were at the end. I searched for and found a music CD in my stack; the great saxophonist

Stan Getz playing songs from Brazil. I sat back reveling in the slow sensuous riffs, sipping warm champagne.

I paged through the dictionary, feeling Vivi's written words string together like a shell necklace around my heart

> *I wait for you in Rio, will take you to the Sugar Loaf and drive you crazy in the arms of Yêmanjá at our beaches and will dance to the sound of Tom Jobim in the Tijuca Forest. Americans are so afraid of pleasure. Pleasure produces energy and happiness! And you, my cat, are Brazilian at heart.*

Charlie padded into the room, stopped, and stared up at me. "Well, what do you think," I said. "Is she The One?"

The cat flicked his tail and meowed.

I kissed the scrap of paper and licked her name.

At sunset, I burst into Mission Control. "That's it! Shut it down!"

"My, my, why the sudden change of heart?" Rathbone said, looking up from a stack of letters.

The TAs all glanced at each other: "VIVI CORREA!"

Wrapped in my cocoon of bliss with the private dancer, my arms flew up into the air. I joyfully samba two-stepped across the room.

"Is he drunk?" Rathbone said.

"Yeah—but not on booze," Kwame said.

"Damn," Ralph said. "One whirl with Miss Brazil and our boy turns into Rico Suave."

"Next thing you know, he'll be moving to South Beach," Steve said.

"NO,*"* I said without interrupting my dance, "I'm going to *REE-OH."*

"Will someone please explain to me what on earth is going on?" Rathbone pleaded.

I continued snapping my fingers and moving my hips, oozing rapture *tropicale.* Ralph described Vivi Correa to Rathbone. Her nationality, occupation, and appearance the day before at Mission Control ending with, "A total bombshell, she blew up the room."

"Yeah," Steve murmured in awe, "imagine what she did to our boy. Look at him. His every atom has been rearranged."

"Damn. He actually has rhythm," Kwame added.

Cocking out a hip and holding the pose, I spun an office chair around and around, then dropped down onto the seat and planted my feet on the ground. "All I can say, gentlemen, is that everything ever said, written, and sung about Brazilian women is only the slightest of approximations. All the raves…mere understatements. And if there are other life forms in our universe or the other gazillion far-flung galaxies, none will ever approach the staggering beauty and luscious, radiant sexuality of the human female form. And if Vivi Correa is any indication, the *última, requintada, muito quente* example of Woman takes up curvaceous, *deliciosa* residence in Rio de Janeiro, Brazil."

I slapped the side of my head with my palm. "Aie! I have never seen such beauty and skills. The taste and smell of her. Her eyes. Her lips! Those hips!! Her chama!"

"One night with her," Steve said, looking around, "and he's fluent in Portuguese."

"What she did with her body, the way her bum bum—oh, hell..." I broke into mad, joyous laughter, and stared straight ahead, reliving Vivi on the screen behind my eyes.

My crazed passion was so contagious that it became group hypnosis. Rathbone and the TAs now also stared off into space as if watching the same movie.

"You know," I continued in a more subdued tone, "that woman is proof positive that racism is ridículo. Put the black and white races together and what do you get? Mulata, the most beautiful woman of them all."

They all nodded, their heads slowly bobbing up and down.

"Enough," Ralph said, smacking his hand down on the table and breaking the spell. "Best thing to do is get right back in the game."

"No way," I said forcefully. "No other woman could ever measure up to her." I jumped to my feet. "I'm here to announce my retirement from the bachelor business." My eyes glazed over again.

"He's got it bad," Kwame said.

Steve waved a hand in front of my face. "Earth to Michael—come in, please." Steve turned to Ralph. "Houston, we've got a problem."

Ralph swiveled the computer screen toward me. "Bathe in the light of this, amigo. Pick a card, any card..."

Earlier, he had framed the pictures of four women in a card deck's suit of hearts. Ralph pointed, "First, we have a gorgeous actress. Second, an adventuress who just kayaked all the way around Greenland. Third, is a female long haul trucker who just called in; she's smokin' hot and approaching the state line. Fourth, the newly crowned Miss Memphis. Here," Ralph said, picking up and placing my hand on the computer mouse, "click on the cards to read their credentials."

Nothing registered. Finally, just to end the pressure and enable me to float back up onto my cloud of bliss with Vivi, I halfheartedly pointed to Miss Memphis because she was out of state, the furthest away. As I glided toward the door, Ralph stuffed a piece of paper with her phone number into my hand.

"Do it, dude. Call her. I'll be all over you tomorrow to make sure you do," he warned.

Back home, I calmed down by taking a long shower, and poured a glass of scotch. I sat at my desk and opened the laptop.

## *THEOREM #5: LIFE AND DEATH*

I keep thinking about something that Vivi Correa wrote in her note: *Americans are so afraid of pleasure. Pleasure produces energy and happiness!* So true...both sentences, but especially the second (even for this Americano). I've never felt so fucking happy and alive! I have endless energy. No need to eat, sleep. I feel truly connected to life and the universe. It's as if I've swallowed the sun.

Wondering why our culture is so afraid of pleasure, I went back to our beginning—Anglo America, and Googled: *Pilgrims and Puritans*. I learned that the Puritans' aim in populating the New World was not only to reform and purify the church, but individual conduct as well…with the Bible the only guide to live by.

Why, on a family vacation to Europe as a boy when I saw my first naked women in Italy and France on prime time television, did nudity in Europe seem as natural and normal as could be, despite my Catholic brainwashing and guilt? Why were the naked male statues fully equipped and front and center in nearly every piazza in Florence, Italy while at home in the U.S. the genitalia of nude statues in public parks were shamefully hidden behind a fig leaf or rendered with a blank spot to begin with?

Touring Peggy Guggenheim's home and art museum in Venice, Italy, our guide explained that in the courtyard there was a Mario Marini sculpture of a nude, ecstatic male sitting astride a horse and the rider had more than his arms extended straight out. Seems that due to the near-unanimous shock of many American visitors, Ms. Guggenheim had the rider's penis made removable (able to be screwed in and out). Whenever American guests were on site, the statue was sans penis.

Why in our culture is it shameful to show a functioning penis, bare female breast, or the beauty of a man and woman making love, but it's perfectly normal to watch someone's head getting blown off every four seconds in movies, television, and the ever-present video games, with the shells flipping from the clip in glorified slow motion?

To get us in the U.S. to tune in, there's a saying in TV newsrooms, "If a story bleeds, it leads." What does that say about Americans that we find entertainment in watching murders and brutalities? Violence to me is what's pornographic, not sex.

The first thing that we see as innocent babies when we open our eyes to this world are rose-tipped, voluminous breasts that fill us with creamy pap, giving us our first taste of la dolce vita! And we males want to continue seeing those succulent spheres in all their pulchritudinous, heaving, heavenly glory—providing a man life-long sustenance and joy.

Unless, as my favorite comedian Rodney Dangerfield said, "My mother never breast-fed me as a child. She said she only liked me as a friend." Seriously, why does our culture prefer death and suffering over life and joy?

I think it's because we have been brainwashed to fear wild nature. The word *wilderness* is mentioned three hundred times in the Bible and always in derogatory terms. Sex is the subset of the wild in ourselves. Religion for ages has tried to kill what it can't control.

The Devil didn't exist until the Church turned Pan the lusty Forest God, conveniently equipped with horns and cloven hooves, into Beealzabub. And all the witches burned at the stake in Salem, Massachusetts were merely earth guardians and natural healers who refused to leave nature to worship inside a man-made building. Witch derives from *wicca*, meaning *wise one.*

And along with the wild we fear real freedom. As a 'red devil' once said,

"You call it wild, but it wasn't really wild. It was free. Animals aren't wild, they're just free. And that's the way we were. You called us wild, you called us savages. But we were just free! If we were savages, Columbus would never have gotten off this island alive." —Leon Shenandoah, Onondaga Chief

Vivi and Ellen are modern-day pagan priestesses, wicca, and female sorceresses; they are free with their bodies and more comfortable naked than wearing clothes for they are from foreign cultures. Vivi—Brazil. Ellen—African (at heart). And since black Brazilians originated from Africa, they are, in a sense, sisters

Having sex with Vivi or Ellen is being in a deep, wordless communication. It's as if when we come together our bodies are launching platforms, serving stations flinging our souls into the stratosphere of pure happiness and joy. As much as I love to read and write, I am not that cerebral. I gain more wisdom through my body. I am finding that sex returns me to the wild, animalizes me, restores me to my most instinctual, true, and vital self.

Ellen told me that first time we stayed in bed two days and nights that a man's penis is multi-purpose, used for elimination and procreation. But a woman's clitoris is there for only one reason, pleasure. "Evolution, or the Intelligent Designer, if you will, doesn't make mistakes," she said.

I'm reading *The Soul of Sex* by Thomas Moore. I'll let him have the last words tonight: "Eros is the principle of vitality. When we are behaving and thinking morally we get depressed and life becomes colorless. When it has no roots in eros, the very pulse of life that draws us forward, morality has a deadening effect that tends to spread through families, marriages, and communities. People who choose to live life in its fullness have no choice but to test the limits of accepted morality and often transgress them."

"Will we have the courage to come out from hiding beneath moralism and hypocrisy? Probably not, if we don't learn to educate for deep values or courage of heart... We are attached to our moralisms because they protect us from the rich possibilities of life."

# 13

# Magnolia Blossoms

**Lee Ann Wells**

**Species Name:** *Feminina Romantikiss*

**Habitat & Range:** Fragrant woodlands across the American South.

**Identifying Characteristics:** Slow-drawl call. Long legs, rosy breast, pearly-white overbite.

**Best Known For:** Instantaneous pair bonding.

The next afternoon, when I returned from the gym, the message light was blinking on the phone. It was Ralph, "You know that *Jeremiah Johnson* movie you're always after us to watch? Well, I saw it last night. And in the words of a wild and wooly mountain man, if ya don't call Miss Memphis, I'm gonna slit ya from crotch to eyeball with a dull deer antler. Get on the horn, Jeremiah, and call her!"

To protect my innards and to try out a new tough love approach I'd been thinking about to scare women away, I grabbed the phone and punched in Lee Ann Wells' number. She answered.

After exchanging a few pleasantries, she said: "Mah-kal, Ah just have to see yew."

"But Lee Ann, you don't even know me. What if I'm a serial killer?"

"Then I'll dah happy!"

I shook my head and couldn't help but grin. So much for tough love I liked her sense of humor and that accent was so beguiling. "Have you been to New York before?" I said.

"Yes, and I have lots of frequent fliah miles."

"All right, but my treat once you're here."

"Ah'll take the Airporter right to your door. Instead of a pizza delivered, yew'll git Miss Memphis!"

"Lee Ann, you're too much. See you this weekend."

Setting down the phone, I felt stricken with guilt. Cheating already on divine Vivi; I'm on a roller coaster that won't stop...

***

At the appointed hour on Friday evening I was dressed in a navy blue sport coat, white dress shirt, and jeans. After my first date with Shareen, while driving her to the airport she said that a woman's first impression of a man always included two things: his watch and his shoes. So, I went shopping and added a stainless steel TAG Heuer watch and basic black ankle boots from Kenneth Cole to my look.

I paced back and forth in the foyer of the apartment building, burning off nervous energy. *What's happened to my life? Five years in Alaska without a date and now I feel like a kid in a candy shop and the lids are off all the jars. I've turned into a Man-Ho. But these blind dates never get any easier...* I continued pacing and glanced at my watch every thirty seconds.

Finally, the Airporter van screeched to a halt in front of the building. I went down the stairs just as Lee Ann Wells climbed out of the van and turned, facing me on the sidewalk. She was tall, thin, yet curvy with large doe-brown eyes, wavy chestnut hair, and a pert nose. She had a dazzling bright smile with perfect teeth and a slight overbite that for some reason turned me on.

"Even more beautiful than your pictures," I said as she walked closer, "and you smell fantastic! What is it?"

"I travel so much that I had mah aroma therapist whip up a lil' somethin' that reminds me of home," Lee Ann said, turning up a thin, fragrant wrist to my nose.

"Smells like flowers," I said.

She smiled. "Magnolia blossoms."

We went up to my apartment and dropped her bags. "Hungry?" I asked.

She nodded. Standing close and looking directly at me with large eyes I saw her pupils swell. I looked away already feeling a tug on my heart.

We went to La Bella Cuccina, my favorite trattoria on Mulberry Street in Little Italy. It was the real deal with red and white checkered tablecloths, Chianti in basket-bottles, faded paintings of Napoli and Venetian glories on the walls, a permanent aroma of garlic, and old-country, white-aproned waiters there since the first day the place opened. Sinatra and Dino crooned songs of happy and sad amoré over the antiquated sound system.

All heads turned to Lee Ann as we entered. The energy lifted in the room as we were seated at a table by the window looking out on Mulberry Street that was so often a movie set.

"I can't believe I'm really here with yew. Such a famous author and Mister Cosmo and all."

"You? I can't believe I'm with a real beauty queen."

"It's just little ole Memphis. I have mah sights set a lot higher."

Lee Ann Wells was the first bona fide southern belle I had ever met and her beauty and ultra-femininity slayed me. Trying to regain a semblance of control I blurted, "Don't you find beauty pageants demeaning?"

"No, not at all. They are talent contests and after a win yew get a scholarship to further your education. Since I've won Miss Memphis, I now want to be Miss Tennessee, then Miss America."

"What about the swimsuit part?"

"Honestly," she said, leaning forward. "I just don't get all the fuss. The good Lord gave us all a body and why should we be ashamed of it?"

Deciding to show my hand, I waved my napkin as if to cool myself down. "What is it about you southern belles?"

"What evah du yew mean?" she accentuated her honey-dripping accent, then tilted her head and batted her big brown eyes.

"See…we men don't stand a chance."

Ah, yew're so sweet! Well, it really is that as little girls when we're standing at the sink washing dishes with Mama, she teaches us all about you men. I'm not gonna give away all the secrets, but unlike these Yankee girls," she paused to glance around, then whispered, "we know how to be a woman and how to please a man."

"Waiter. Check, please!" I said with no waiter in sight.

She giggled. "Yew're so funny! I didn't expect ya to be so nice."

The whole world closed down to just the woman sitting across from me. The food arrived. We started with salty prosciutto wrapped around sweet melon, moved on to baked ziti and a crunchy risotto, and then dug wholeheartedly into Abruzzo angel hair pasta smothered in green basil, pungent sage, and topped with a blizzard of freshly-grated parmigiano reggiano. We washed it all down with a bottle of Famiglia Anselma Barolo wine with tantalizing berry flavors and a nose full of roses, pausing our lively conversation to pass plates back and forth and clink our glasses together. We continued the feast with pistachio and lemon gelatos—reaching across the table with our spoons to wipe gobs of the creamy flavors on each other's tongues, and then sprinted to the finish with double espressos that could wake the dead or resuscitate the stuffed.

Back at my apartment we enjoyed a nightcap. Talk and laughter came easily to us. When the drinks were finished, I stood up and said, "Lee Ann, I'm sorry. We didn't even talk about a hotel or sleeping arrangements. Why don't you take the bed and I'll grab my sleeping bag and camp on the couch."

She reached up and caught me by the belt buckle. "Mahkal, I didn't flah a thousand miles to sleep all by mahself!" Lee Ann stood up, stepped into me and laid a kiss on my lips as slow and sweet as molasses.

"Just give me a few minutes," she said, picking up her suitcase. "I'll call yew when I'm ready." She swayed toward the bedroom, smiling over her shoulder.

I collapsed onto the couch. *I think I finally have it figured out. I was a priest in a past life who somehow managed to remain celibate and this is the reward for my chastity.*

I heard her call. "Yew can come in now."

It took my eyes a moment to adjust to the darkness, then I saw Lee Ann in bed, the blankets up to her neck. She grabbed the corner of the covers and slowly pulled them down until she lay there completely nude.

"What's the mattah?" she whispered. "You look like you've never seen a naked woman before."

As I worshipped with my eyes, a line from the great sculptor Rodin sprang to mind.

"A penny for your thoughts," she said.

"A woman undressing is like the sun breaking through the clouds."

"Ahhw." She then curled an index finger toward her.

I quickly undressed and slid into bed beside her. She swung over on her side—the blankets billowing down around us. Her high-beam eyes were inches away and then our kisses melted time. I honored her breasts with my mouth, nudged her onto her back and slowly moved down.

She suddenly burst into tears.

My head snapped up. "What? Did I do something wrong?"

"No, that's the problem."

"What's the problem?"

"I'm already fallin' in love with yew!" she cried.

I was stunned and at a total loss as to what to say or do. I got up and brought her a Kleenex.

"Take me to the airport now, please."

"What?"

"NOW," she sobbed.

"Lee Ann, I'll go sleep on the couch like I said I was going…"

"No, now!

"OK. But I don't want to leave you stranded all alone at the airport in the middle of the night."

"I'll be all right."

"Are you sure you want to leave now?"

"Yes."

We dressed in silence and I called a cab. We rode to the airport with only the sound of Lee Ann snuffling. Finally I said, "Lee Ann, are you involved with someone?"

"No." She started crying again. "It's jus' that I have to concentrate on mah career right now and you are Mister Bachelor and why should you give all that up for me and it never works long distance and oh, I'm so confused!"

The cab stopped at the Departures curb at LaGuardia Airport. We sat in silence for a few moments. I waited for her to say something or change her mind. I started to open my door to get out.

"Don't," she said. She leaned over, kissed me on the cheek and was gone.

I slumped in the seat as the cab zoomed back to the city. Tears welled up in my eyes. *Must be contagious.* I forcefully shook my head, trying to reboot my brain. *So fast and furious, can't even get over one without another... It's like I'm powerless. How am I ever going to choose just one when each woman is so damned GLORIOUS!* I saw Lee Ann in my bed again and then our children with beautiful eyes and perfect overbites. We'd all speak with southern accents and live in a big house with tall white pillars and lead graceful, charmed lives.

Back inside my apartment, I twisted the cork top from the bottle of scotch and took a long chug. I stepped into the bedroom. *DAMMIT.* I turned and dug my sleeping bag out of the closet and unrolled it on the couch. My bed smelled too much of magnolia blossoms.

I stopped by Mission Control the following evening. The TAs were sorting through a new day's mail deliveries.

"Hey. How was Miss Memphis?" Ralph said. They dropped what they were doing and huddled around me.

I filled them in. "So much for the theory that *Cosmo* girls are all going to be no-strings adventuresses."

"Women use sex to get love; men use love to get sex. That's what my wife says," Steve said.

"But I never used the *L* word!" I lamented.

"You don't have to, bro," Kwame said.

"What do you mean?"

Ralph nodded. "Hell, man…if I was a woman, I'd want your babies."

I groaned.

# 14

# No Viagra Needed

I walked into the gym at Chelsea Piers, a temple to fitness, and stopped. Sipping wheat grass at the brushed-aluminum bar was a man who had to be sixty yet was a colossus, cut and ripped from lifting tons of weights and doing intense cardio. In-between my own lifting efforts, I often stood at the back of the gym to rest at the tall glass wall where I could watch this senior bull beat the young bucks at racquetball. I approached this titan and introduced myself.

"Johnny O'Reilly," the man said in a deep baritone and clutched my hand in an iron-clad grip.

"I admire you so much. I've seen you work out. Do you mind if I ask your age?"

"Turned seventy-five last week."

"No way. I had you at sixty tops." I shook my head slowly in amazement and admiration.

"Well, I've been coming here every day for years."

"It shows. Seventy-five! Wow. You're the man I want to be. Can I join you?"

"Sure."

I ordered a Blueberry Blitz protein smoothie and sat down. "What got you started working out?"

"Once upon a time just after the dinosaurs ruled the earth, I was an actor. Did bit and character parts off-Broadway and sometimes on. In those days we didn't have all the fancy microphones and sound systems like now. You had to be able to project your voice to the back row. I knew I had to stay strong if I was going to make a career of it so I started hitting the weights and running. Distance and resistance—not only made me stronger, but smarter, too. Could memorize a script page with one glance. I read awhile back that exercise not only strengthens the muscles, but also sends glycogen up to the brain. The ancient Greeks had it right about the mind-body connection."

"What was your favorite role?" I asked eagerly.

"Well, my one claim to fame was when Jason Robards as Hickey in *The Iceman Cometh* went down for two weeks with laryngitis and I stepped in."

"Maybe I saw you. My parents took me to the theater all the time."

"What do you do?"

I explained, giving the short form of a reply.

Johnny slapped me on the back. "You got life by the tail, son. Women are the reason for getting out of bed in the morning and back in at night."

"Ever married?"

"Yes, I was blessed by the love of a wonderful wife. Gracie died of cancer a few years ago. I was lucky. We had forty great years together and four kids, older than you now, all with good careers and families of their own."

"From your experience what would you say is the biggest difference between men and women?"

O'Reilly sipped his wheat grass thinking for a moment. "My fellow Irishman Oscar Wilde said it best: 'A man wants to be a woman's first love; a woman a man's last.'. They live to get a hold and make a project out of us. Love is everything to most women; to a man—it's just one part of life."

"What about now, are you seeing anyone?"

"*Ha!*" He leaned forward. "I have more girlfriends than you can shake a dick at."

"So it never stops, huh?"

"Not if you stay in shape. My next door neighbor, Jack, let himself go. He's about forty to fifty pounds overweight and with all the B.S. that comes with it—heart trouble, diabetes, a pecker that comes and goes. He has an on-and-off again girlfriend. He's always complaining, *What I used to do all night, now takes me all night to do.* Not me. I wake up every morning with a hard-on a cat couldn't scratch!"

I took a moment to move my mind around that staunch image. "Where do you meet women?"

"In my apartment building here and the condo I keep in a big complex in Florida. Nearly all of them are widows. Live long enough, kid, and you'll be in even higher demand. I'm their handyman. I'm even thinking of starting a new business: Rent-A-Hubby, for all the things I'm forever fixing for them." Johnny grinned. "The pay is terrible, but the fringe benefits are great. The ones that stay in shape with golf or tennis are still prime-trim and lonely as hell. Let's just say that I screw in more than light bulbs."

"So it never tapers off?"

"Are you kidding? My dad lived to be ninety-four, but unfortunately toward the end I had to put him in a nursing home. I got a call in the middle of the night to rush over there. Seems one of the staff heard a bunch of commotion coming from his room. They go in and see Pop with his diaper down getting a blow job from some eighty-year-old gal. Or should I say *gum job.* She took her teeth out before diving in."

"That's nasty!" I said, cringing.

"Tell you a secret, son. Something I've never told anyone else."

I leaned in.

"I went outside my marriage one time. And, strangely, I just couldn't feel bad when I saw all the good it did."

"How so?"

"I was acting off-Broadway. One of my first gigs. There was a girl from the Midwest in the same play. After the shows, we started going out for a drink. She was pasty-faced, about twenty pounds overweight, slouched over, apologizing for being alive. Men never paid her any attention. But, from time to time, I saw a spark of passion in her eyes when she talked about the theater and literature. Well, one night we ended up back at her place. One thing led to another and the floodgates opened. She was insatiable. Two, three times a day."

"She lost thirty pounds, outran me in the New York City Marathon, tailored her clothes to fit, and was suddenly *sex walking*. You wouldn't believe it was the same woman. She was switched on, lit up, fully juiced. Her career took off like a shot. And I had endless exalted energy—like I had life itself by the tail. Happiness flowed off me. And everywhere I went, it didn't matter—women came at me left and right, jumping into my space like they were feeding on a contact high."

"Sounds like *Sexual Healing*, that Marvin Gaye song," I told him.

"Yep," O'Reilly nodded. "Greatest medicine there is. I saw pure animal lust transform two people and much of the world around us for the better."

"But what about adultery being a sin?"

"If man makes it, don't eat it."

"What?" I didn't understand.

"Ever hear of Jack LaLanne?"

"Sure. The fitness guru. You remind me of him."

"Thanks. He's my hero…still a stud at ninety. Jack was being interviewed by Larry King and Larry asked him of all the diets out there today, what works best? Jack said, "If man makes it, don't eat it." I think it's the same with religion. If you pulled back the curtain on all these religions, like the Wizard of Oz, you'd see hypocrites and charlatans manipulating the controls."

From a TV mounted on the wall an announcer blurted: "See a doctor for erections lasting longer than four hours..." We turned to the TV and saw a middle-aged couple holding hands.

Once again I thought, *Animal show: Walrus oosik. Permanent penile bone. Reaches two feet in length. A built-in boner. No Viagra needed. When the weather is frigid, the walrus is rigid.*

O'Reilly drained the last of his wheat grass. "Now that I'm closer to the end of the trail, looking back—what I think about most isn't the money I made or the acting roles I played. I think about the joy of women and carnal delights."

"Why do you think that is?"

"Because, son, women are life—to the highest degree. Hearing a woman's love song, those squeals of delight, is like music from the gods. I read somewhere, I think it was the French philosopher Gilles Néret, who said, 'the only real antidote to man's awareness of his inevitable death is erotic joy.' For me, morality is simple. Good is whatever increases the life force. Bad is whatever diminishes it. Society can try all it wants to stomp it out of you, but never lose the lust, kid. It's the fountain of youth and the fuel that runs the engine of the universe. Lust puts the sap in the trees and the pep in your step. I wake up every morning with a reminder of what I was put on earth for. We're men. It wakes up before we do. It's nature's way. The male plug inserts into the female socket that rockets and electrifies life. Pull those two apart and what do you got? No juice, no power. Trust in lust and you'll be a happy man."

He crumpled the empty wheat grass cup between two fingers and asked me, "You want to hear my favorite poem?"

"Sure."

"It's by Theodore Roethke," he said, standing up. He turned to face the gym and in a booming baritone began:

"I knew a woman, lovely in her bones.
When small birds sighed, she would sigh back at them;
Ah, when she moved, she moved more ways than one:
The shapes a bright container can contain!
Of her choice virtues only gods should speak,
Or English poets who grew up on Greek
(I'd have them sing in chorus, cheek to cheek.)

How well her wishes went! She stroked my chin,
She taught me Turn, and Counter-turn, and stand;
She taught me Touch, that undulant white skin:
I nibbled meekly from her proffered hand;
She was the sickle; I, poor I, the rake,
Coming behind her for her pretty sake
(But what prodigious mowing did we make.)

Love likes a gander, and adores a goose:
Her full lips pursed, the errant note to seize;
She played it quick, she played it light and loose;
My eyes, they dazzled at her flowing knees;
Her several parts could keep a pure repose,
Or one hip quiver with a mobile nose
(She moved in circles, and those circles moved.)

Let seed be grass, and grass turn into hay:
I'm martyr to a motion not my own;
What's freedom for? To know eternity.
I swear she cast a shadow white as stone.
But who would count eternity in days?
These old bones live to learn her wanton ways:
(I measure time by how a body sways.)'"

Everyone in the gym set down their weights and applauded.

Johnny O'Reilly turned, winked at me, and a man of near-oosik proportions strode away—leaving me to admire him for the colossus that he was.

# 15

## "Be the Woman."

**<u>Orlando</u>**
**Species Name:** *Michali Genderbenderitis*
**Habitat & Range:** Lesbian bars.
**Identifying Characteristics:** Drop dead gorgeous.
**Best Known For:** Being male enough to be female.

When I returned home from the gym and opened my door, there was a manila envelope on the floor. Opening it, I read:

> *This woman will NOT self-destruct in five seconds. —Mission Control*
> *P.S. Kwame said to tell you: Once you go Asian, you'll never go Caucasian!*

I read about Suki Abadesco: Image Consultant... Filipina... Ex-Marine... Runner... Black belt in Taekwondo.

I fed Charlie, grabbed a beer from the refrigerator, then sat at the kitchen table and looked at her picture. Long blue-black hair, dusky skin, dark sharp-cut eyes, feminine, yet firmly muscled. I lifted the phone.

"Hallo." Her voice was sultry and alluring.

"Hi," I said, running both feet up and down under the table. "This is Michael, the…"

"I knew you would call."

"Oh, really?"

"Yes. There are some things you need to know."

My feet hit the floor and stopped. "Such as?" I asked warily.

"Come over and we'll talk about it."

"When?"

"Tomorrow, but come early in the afternoon and leave your night free."

"And what makes you think there are things I need to know?"

"From looking at your picture and now hearing your voice."

The next day, I found myself standing next to Suki Abadesco admiring black and white photographs of female nudes on the walls of her living room.

"Aren't they beautiful?" Suki said. "This is my favorite curve." A long red fingernail traced an upraised flared hip.

"Mine, too," I said. "Where God lives." I stopped looking at the pictures and stared hard at Suki.

"What?" she said.

"Just, well…I've never looked at naked women with a woman before. Nice—this mutual admiration."

She smiled.

"Just read that eighty percent of all the pictures on the internet are of naked women. Why do you think that is?"

"We're the sexier sex. Men and women want women. I made a pitcher of martinis. Have a seat. Be right back."

I sat in a chair and waited. The living room was simple but elegant. The walls were painted light gray and a sleek black leather couch was fronted by a clear glass coffee table with a gold bowl full of ripe red pomegranates in the center.

Suki returned with a tray that she placed on the coffee table. She handed me a large glass with a long stem and from a metal beaker poured clear chilled liquor. She did the same for herself, and then sat down across from me on the couch.

"Never had a martini before," I said, taking a sip. "Wow. Smooth." I decided to get right to it. "So, what is it that I need to know?"

Suki sipped then set the big glass down. "I'm an image consultant for CEOs, professional athletes, famous actors, politicians. They hire me to tell them how best to dress, speak…how to get their hair cut."

"Image is perception."

"Yes, totally, in our visually dominated culture."

"And you think I need a makeover?"

"Yes, but not in the ways you might think or what I would normally do."

I set down the drink. "I'm confused."

"I'm also a clairvoyant, inherited it from my mother. She is a very famous *curandera* in the Philippines. It's probably what makes me so good at my day job. No matter what changes you make on the outside they aren't effective unless you first change what's going on here." She placed a hand over her heart.

"And what did you see from my picture or hear in my voice that convinces you I need changing?"

"As long as you remain an outsider you'll never truly understand what it is you are seeking."

"And what might that be?"

"Women and how to love them."

I stared into Suki's eyes, then nodded warily.

"You are too rigid, too male—too *yang* in your beliefs. You need to shake things up to gain a new perspective."

"And how do I do that?"

"You need to come from the inside-out instead of the outside looking in."

"Give it to me in practical terms."

"Dress up as a woman and go to a lesbian bar."

My mouth fell open. "NO WAY."

"I read your book. Remember how after you tangled with the grizzly bear you then felt at one with it and empowered? It's because you had the attitude: Be the Bear. Now—be the Woman."

Every fiber of my body was squirming, rebelling, even though in a deeper soulful place I was intrigued. "So, what do you charge for this image makeover?"

"Nothing—if you'll be my date for the evening?"

"You're serious."

Suki nodded and flashed a smile.

I picked up the martini and took a long sip. Then I looked at her through a Clint Eastwood *High Plains Drifter* squint. "Two conditions, doll."

"Yes?"

"No pictures and no talking to the press."

"You have my word."

I drained the glass and held it up. With clenched jaw I hissed through my teeth, "OK. I'm your girl—as long as you make us another pitcher of these, please."

"Very well. While I'm doing that go into the bathroom *Dirty Harry*. Fill the tub with hot water and bubble bath. Take off your clothes and get in.

Clint flinched.

"Chop, chop. We've got a lot of work to do. You just might be man enough to be a woman."

"Hurry up with those drinks before I exercise a woman's prerogative."

"Which is?"

"Changing my mind."

I followed instructions, glad there were foaming bubbles to hide under. She knocked.

"OK," I said.

She entered with two fresh martinis and lit candles around the room. She reached into a drawer and approached me with a gleaming straight-edge razor.

She made a lifting motion with her hand.

"What?"

"Leg, please."

"What? No way."

I watched with horror and amazement as my right leg lifted, seemingly of its own accord.

"You sure you know how to use that thing?"

"Yes. It gives the closest shave."

She sat on the edge of the tub and shaved me in steady, upward strokes.

Reaching the top of my thigh, she stopped and handed me the razor. "You do the meat and potatoes."

"The wha… Oh, no..."

She shrugged and continued.

"I read that you were a Marine. Active duty?"

"Yes, the Gulf War. I was a tank commander."

"Why am I not surprised..."

She shampooed my hair, slowly massaging the scalp. I surrendered, leaning back and closing my eyes. After the conditioner, she rinsed my head with handfuls of fresh water from the bath tap.

I picked up the martini. "Delicious. An icy martini in a hot bath..." I held up the glass.

She took it, sipped, and shaved my arm. With both arms done, she slid forward on the top edge of the tub. Facing me, she shaved my chest and then my face and neck.

"I don't believe this," I murmured carefully. "And God, you're beautiful."

"What don't you believe?"

"Well, an hour ago we were total strangers and now this—you wielding a straight-edge razor, no less. And the strangest thing is I feel totally comfortable with you, like somehow I've known you before and we're just meeting again."

"Maybe in a past life I was the husband and you were my wife."

I slid underwater. Suki reached down into the bubbles and pulled me up by the ear.

"I think I know what it is that makes you attractive," she said.

"What?"

"Underneath the rippling hunk is a raging nerd."

"Yeah, after Alaska my pecs may be bigger, but I still wear a pocket protector."

"Don't lose it. The nerd is what keeps the hunk from being a *bimbo.* "

"You've done this before, haven't you?"

"What?"

"Turned men into women. Isn't there a goddess in *The Odyssey* who did the same thing?"

"You're thinking of Circe," she said, while shaving near my ear. "She turned men into swine."

"Oh."

"Most men today don't require her powers of conversion."

"Suki?"

"What."

"You're not weird or anything, are you? Like some psycho serial killer that lures men into a bubble bath before..."

"Before what?"

"Hacking off their meat and potatoes."

"I thought you said you felt comfortable with me." She sat back, razor uplifted.

I exhaled. "Sorry. Just that the straight-edge is a wicked weapon and when it went out of sight there for a couple seconds, I flashed on Lorena Bobbitt. So, you don't often turn men into women?"

"Just the one who needs it the most."

I grabbed her wrist.

"Yes?"

"Be honest…I'm not one of many?"

Our eyes locked. She grinned. "This is good. You're already feeling what a woman often feels."

"What?"

"Worried about being *one of many*."

I nodded slowly, thinking I might learn something after all.

She stood up and turned her back to me. "Now, stand up. Shower off all the loose hair and foam. Put on a towel. I'll be right back."

I did as told. She knocked. "Decent?"

"Yes."

She walked to the toilet and closed the lid. "Sit here."

"What now?"

"Phase Two."

She reached above me to a shelf covered with tubes and jars. She picked out a jar and unscrewed the lid. She dabbed the moisturizer onto my legs, arms, and chest and rubbed it in. "Thirsty skin."

"What's in that one?" I looked over my shoulder at a lone concoction on the bottom shelf. "TNS," I read. "Sort of has an aura around it."

"Best treatment there is for your face. My skin lady sold it to me after my last facial."

"What is it?"

"Stem cells from circumcised foreskins."

"You're kidding."

"No, latest thing. All the rage. It totally rejuvenates the skin."

I shook my head. "I wish Rodney was still alive."

"Who?"

"My favorite old-school comedian, Rodney Dangerfield, would have had a field day with that. *My wife goes for a facial. They rub on a lotion made of stem cells from circumcised foreskins. She cheated on me with a newborn! Gives new meaning to getting a "little head."*"

Suki laughed. "You're quick." She led me into the bedroom. I sat at a vanity with my back to the mirror and she studied my face for a long moment like an artist looking at a blank canvas.

"You want to be blonde, brunette, or redhead?" she said, stepping away to open a closet door. There on shelves were a dozen wigs perched on Styrofoam heads.

"Why so many?"

"I lived with a woman for three years. After the heat was gone, we dressed up—cheated on each other with each other."

"Still together?"

"No, she left me for someone new."

"So, even with women love doesn't last," I said sadly.

"*Me so horny, me love you long time*," Suki quoted from the movie *Full Metal Jacket*. "I think love was invented to fool us. People behave better with their friends than those whom they live with or love. Love comes with impossible expectations. If we were just friends with benefits that would work best and last longest."

"Never thought of it in those terms. You might be right."

"Maybe a brunette your first time out. So you can blend in and not call too much attention to yourself."

"No, I want that purple bee-hive up there. So Amy Winehouse."

We laughed.

"I like you, Michael."

"I like you, too."

For the next half-hour, Suki slowly made up my face, applying powders and paint with an assortment of smooth brushes that flicked and fluttered. "So sensuous," I said.

"If you want any more to drink, do it now. Once the lipstick goes on that's it until we get to the bar."

We took a break and sipped our martinis.

"Where are we going?"

"Mister Sister."

"Great name. Ask you something?"

"Sure."

"When you lost your virginity was it with a girl or a boy?"

"It happened with a girl in college. I was a total LUG: *Lesbian Until Graduation*. Didn't have anything to do with men until later."

"What made you change your mind?"

"It was not so much him, but where we did it. I was on vacation in Florida. Met this guy in a bar and we left and got stoned in his car, then we laid down right on the side of some train tracks. He knew there was a train coming. We started in on each other, kissing and shit and the ground started shaking and just when the engine was nearly on us, we both came and rolled away down the embankment. Best orgasm of my life."

"Wow. The earth really moved."

"Yeah, but now I want it just man, no train. Hold still."

She held up a gold tube. She twisted it and a pink, pointed bullet appeared. She smeared the color on my lips. "Go like this...she rubbed her lips together.

I aped her movements. "Damn. Everything is so soft and sensuous. Steve Martin was right."

"About what?"

"He said if he were a woman he would just stay home all day and play with himself."

"Like Howard Stern always going on about how he's *a lesbian trapped in a man's body.*"

"Yeah."

"Well, lesbians take offense to that, but then they take offense at most everything that's het."

"Het?"

"Heterosexual. Do you know who invented lipstick?"

"No."

"Cleopatra. It's a sex signal."

"How so?"

"Duplicating her red puffy pussy lips—on her face."

I raised the back of a hand toward my mouth.

"Don't you dare," Suki smiled. "Actually Cleopatra just popularized it. She copied it from prostitutes."

I nodded. "I had a biology professor in college who said everything we do, no matter how far afield, is for one reason: to get laid—propagate the species."

She turned away and applied something to her face. She whirled around. "What about lip gloss. You like?"

"You're killin' me. Not only are they thick and red, but now shiny wet!" I shook my head. "We don't stand a chance. Do women know what they do to us men with all these weapons?"

"Sure."

"Then why when we hit on you do you so readily blow us off?"

"As they say in flight school—it's all about the approach," she explained.

"It kills me at the gym when women walk by with those words printed across the backsides of their shorts: *PINK* or *JUICY*. I know *PINK* is advertising a Victoria's Secret line and *JUICY* is Juicy Couture but come on they're right there, boldfaced across their asses. My favorite not selling anything is *GOOD LUCK*."

"Well, if you want something noticed, put it where guys are looking all the time," she laughed.

"What if we had words across the front of *our* shorts?"

"What would they be?"

I thought for a moment. "*WISH YOU WERE HERE*."

"Words not needed. We get hit with that all the time."

"Ask you something else?"

"Sure."

"Do you prefer men or women?"

"Depends entirely on the person, not the sex. Now, let's get some nails on you."

I watched hands that not long ago were swollen and calloused from chopping wood, catching big fish, and punching a grizzly bear now becoming girly smooth and neatly tipped with acrylic nails.

She set down the glue and picked up two small, squat bottles. "Which color do you want, *Shanghai Shimmer* or *Fuchsia Fandango*?"

"Ya got me."

"*Shanghai*."

She shook the bottle as I extended my fingers and she flicked the pink color on.

"What about pick-up lines? Ready?" I asked. "Tony Montana, from *Scarface*: *Did ju fall in love or do ju want mah to walk by ju again?* Or how about, *Remember mah* name—'*cause ju be screamin' it later*."

She rolled her eyes.

"*Tha only ting that luks good on mah—is ju*."

She shook her head, suppressing a grin. "Want to know the pick-up line that works best?"

"What?"

"Hello."

"Oh, that easy, huh?"

"No, that sincere," she told me.

"You know, the other day I went to the mall. I entered Macy's on the women's side and all these women were sitting in chairs having their makeup done."

"Uh-huh..." she said, standing back, hands on hips, smiling at me. "Sure you didn't sit down with them?"

"Come on. This is my first and last time doing this."

"Just kidding, go on."

"There were like a hundred women all having makeovers. I don't know what got into me, but I impulsively stopped alongside an older gal who clearly had lived a few years. I said to the makeup girl, 'It's impossible to make her look any more beautiful than she already is.' I turned and walked away. But the woman melted behind me and mewed like a kitten—you know that sound women make when you somehow touch their hearts—*AahhHHLLL*. The way the sound keeps rising to the end..."

"Yeah, and you know what? I might have actually gotten up and followed you on that line."

"Really?"

"Really…everything about it was perfect. First, you were sincere. Second, you said it indirectly. Not to the woman herself, but to the girl helping her. And then you walked away wanting nothing from either of them."

Under my makeup, I beamed.

She paused to put away the nail polish bottle. "Tell you a secret. Every woman, no matter how beautiful—even super-model gorgeous—is insecure about her looks or her body."

"No way. Not you."

"Yes, me! Especially me."

"But you're perfect! A twelve out of ten."

"*Ha.* I hate my thighs, too muscular. No matter how much I diet they never go down."

Holding out my hands and gazing with admiration at my newly painted nails I said, "For me, it's my calves. No matter how I bomb them at the gym on the step-up machine, they never get any bigger. Oh, God..."

"What?"

"I've totally crossed over now," I laughed.

"How so?"

"We're having intimate Girl Talk about our body parts!"

"Yeah, you're in-country now, soldier—embedded with the 101st Insecure Division. Man up."

We laughed.

"Who do you think gets the most pleasure from sex: men or women?" I inquired.

"Women, by far. Men only have so many shots in the gun. A woman can string orgasms together like firecrackers on the Fourth of July. Women's sex drive is stronger. We're just better at hiding it. Wrists, please."

I extended both arms and flipped them over.

"Hey, you're getting good at this."

"Yeah. Yeah. The only thing keeping me from running out the front door is a saying."

"What?"

*"The lion, sure of his strength, is therefore very gentle."*

She sprayed *Obsession* perfume behind my paws, up on both sides of my neck and down behind my knees. "You want to hit the pulse points."

She brushed back my hair then walked over to the open closet and took down a shoulder-length brunette wig, wavy with bangs. She fitted it on my head and clipped it in place. With a narrow brush she flipped and fluffed. She stood back. "My, my…"

"Should I look now?"

"No, not yet. Let's do the clothes."

She walked across the bedroom and opened another door. She stepped in and I followed and gave a long whistle. We were in a space nearly as large as the bedroom. Hundreds of dresses, skirts, and blouses hung in order around the perimeter. In the center were free-standing, blonde-wood cabinets filled with drawers of varying heights and topped with trays holding mounds of jewelry, hair clips, and an assortment of feminine accoutrements. Under the clothes, shoe boxes were stacked with a Polaroid picture glued to the end of each box, showing the contents inside.

"In my business, I have to be my own advertisement—dress for success."

"Or sex." I walked over to a row of short dresses in crayon-bright colors. "Are they what I…" My fingers slid over thin rubber as smooth as silk. "*Whoa.* These are wild. Hey, I've got an idea. I pick you what you wear tonight and you choose mine."

"OK."

I looked at rubber dress after dress: candy-apple red, neon-purple, hot-pink. I then stopped at a black latex number with chopped white lace across the front.

"This one," I said removing it from the rack and handing it over.

"Funny you should choose that. Exactly what I planned on wearing. It's a Helmut Lang, only ninety-nine made. Got it in a trade for a consultation."

"Killer. But it looks so tight. How do you get it on?"

"Talcum powder."

"Seriously?"

"Yeah, it's like a wet suit and when it's hot, believe me, rubber is not the thing to wear. But it's what—late November now, cold night like this it's the sexiest feeling on earth the way it hugs every curve like a second skin."

"I…ah…take it you don't wear anything underneath."

She smiled. "My turn..." Suki tugged open a cabinet drawer loaded with lingerie. "You *are* wearing underwear and I want you in these." She held up black silk stockings in one hand and black panties and a lacy garter belt in the other.

I shrugged nonchalantly. "What the hell. In this deep, I might as well go the *full monty*. What about on top?"

"I'm looking."

With Suki preoccupied, I dropped the towel around my waist, stepped into the panties and pulled them up. "I was a chick once before."

"Oh, yeah. When?"

I sat down in a chair. I slipped my feet into the bunched stockings and then unrolled them up my clean-shaven legs. "Until Week Six in the womb. We all start out as girls."

"Then you'll know what to do with this," she said, tossing me a garter belt.

I held it out like a spider. She showed me how to put it on and snapped the tips of the dangling bands onto the tops of the stockings. "You have big pecs, so here, this bra should fit."

I slid my arms through the openings and she hooked it closed in back. She went to the far wall and selected a midnight-blue silk dress with slits up the sides. She then glanced over the shoe box pictures and reached in and pulled out black pumps.

"Not too much heel your first time out or your walk will give you away."

I put on the dress and stepped into the shoes. She gave me jewelry, then stood back and shook her head.

"What?"

"You're going to get hit on more than me."

I laughed.

"Go look in the mirror; let me get dressed."

I stepped into the bedroom and quickly turned around. *Not ready for the mirror just yet.* In awe, I sat down on the edge of the bed and deconstructed myself an article of clothing at a time, staring at and touching what gave me such strange sensations. I stood up and walked in a clomping manner to the left edge of the mirror. I closed my eyes and side-stepped to the front of the glass. I opened my eyes.

For the first time in a mirror, I saw someone other than myself. My eyes looked back at me, but that was all that was the same. My hardness, edges, and armor were gone. Suki had not only worked magic with makeup, but somehow she had found my feminine self and brought it up to the surface.

"HEY," I called.

"Out in a minute..."

"YOU DID AN INCREDIBLE JOB!"

"You like?"

I pursed my lips and blew upward. My bangs lifted in the wind. *Hell, if I don't recognize me, maybe no one else will...*

I practiced walking. Three steps forward and I lost my balance and toppled to the floor. Suki opened the closet door and stood over me.

"Wow," I said. "Careful you don't melt that rubber dress. You are smokin' hot!"

"Thank you. Catch a heel?" She held out both hands, leaned back, and pulled me up.

"Yeah. Suki, you are gorgeous."

"The trick is to lead with your toes like you're putting out a cigarette. That lifts the heel."

I practiced and soon had the hang of it. "What about my voice?"

"Raise it a bit, but not too much. Sultry is sexy."

"Like yours."

"So, how do you feel?"

"Open, vulnerable. Hey, I need a name. How about Michelle?"

She wrinkled her nose. "Too vanilla. *Orlando*—that's who you are."

"Orlando. Why Orlando?"

"Read the novel. Ready?"

"I think so, but next to you I suddenly feel like Paul Bunyan."

"Oh, stop. You look great."

Inside Mister Sister, Suki and Orlando took the last two seats at the bar. The place was packed with women: lipstick lesbians, bull dykes, straight, bent, tall, fat—the full range of the feminine gender drinking, dancing, standing, talking, smoking, swaying, kissing while k.d. lang's new CD played over the speakers.

"Are you seeing what I'm seeing?" Suki said, handing me a martini.

"What?"

"Everyone is checking you out big-time."

"No!"

"Yes! You pass. You are a hot babe."

"Don't know if I should be proud of that or not," I said.

"I went to hear a lecture once by Christine Jorgenson. She was the first man to ever have a sex change operation. She said that everyone is a mix of male and female hormones and emotions and the happiest people manage to integrate both. She said most of us are sixty-forty, with one sex over the other. In her case she felt eighty-twenty female, but in a man's body, so she had the sex change."

"I read that they don't cut off the penis, but invert it."

"Yes, the tissue is much the same. And think of D.H. Lawrence, Henry James, or Milan Kundera who write so well about women. Even the imagination isn't limited by gender."

I nodded. "When Hillary and Norgay first climbed Everest there was a reporter, James Morris, at base camp covering it all. I bought his book. Then he had a sex change and became the famous travel writer, Jan Morris. I went to a book signing and put on the table *his* first book and *her* first one. She signed them both without batting an eye."

"Did she sign the Everest book James or Jan?"

"James, even though he's now Jan."

"See. Be proud; be both."

We looked around the room together. "It's really not much different than in the het world," she said. "The same rules of attraction and body language apply: eye contact, the hair flip, the strutting walk. See that woman over there?"

I nodded, "Zoologists call it *presenting behavior*. That woman looks just like a Bonobo ape. Head back. Legs out. Hips up and swinging. Only her posterior isn't bare, bright red, and swollen."

"Just wait. It's early."

I grinned. "One thing that's different from a het bar is that the vibe in here is way softer, more subtle and diffuse."

"Guys' eyes are like laser beams; they burn another hole in you. Women look, but without the desperation in their gaze." Suki leaned forward. "The butch behind me wants you."

I glanced over her lowered shoulder and saw a squat, burly woman with a graying crew-cut, jeans, flannel shirt, and bolo tie. "Gawd, she's built like a linebacker for the Packers."

"That's Bernice. She's really sweet. Why don't I just disappear and let you two get…"

"NO! SUKI," I grabbed her rubber sleeve. "Don't you dare leave me."

She burst into laughter. "The man who wrestled bears and killer whales—terrified of a little ole lezzie. You're fresh meat, Orlando, and they all want a piece."

"But, I only want you," I said, looking directly into her eyes.

"Come on..."

We danced, we drank, and talked some more.

"What it all comes down to is this," Suki said. "It's all about mind-meld. Every woman knows that men are after one thing and we know it all our lives from the time we're little girls. If you do the unexpected and ignore that drive, get into her head instead and meld your mind with hers, not as a game, but with total interest and sincerity, she will reward you with sex beyond your wildest dreams. The treasure is inside the chest."

I was silent, letting the wisdom sink in.

"The only happily married couple I know…" she continued, "…I'll never forget what my friend Caren once said: 'When I come home from work and Ted asks me how my day went and he sits down to really listen, giving me his full attention—I'm in heaven!' Most men don't listen. They think listening puts them in a subordinate position. It doesn't take much, but it means everything. For a woman there's nothing more erotic than being understood."

"This is great. Suki?"

"What?"

"Thank you."

"Well, it's very unusual and refreshing meeting a man who's open to learning. Have you always been this way?"

I nodded. "I have to learn something new every fifteen minutes or I'm bored. Before, I spent all my time learning about everything but women. That's my deficiency."

"But, it's not just knowing women. It all starts with what Socrates said, 'Know thyself.' We can't love anyone out here," she extended her arm, "unless we first have the love in here," she touched her chest. "We attract what we are. What we are inside is what we manifest externally."

"Uh-oh..." I said, gazing at my feminine garb.

Suki slugged me on the arm.

"No, I hear you loud and clear. Hey, I have to go to the bathroom. Coming?"

"What?"

"Isn't that something women do—go off to the bathroom together?"

"Yes, but no. You go alone. Work it, girl."

Uneasy, I stepped away from the bar like an untethered astronaut taking his first space walk. Halfway across the room, I watched in fascination as a mannish-looking woman placed a sequence of small gifts in front of her paramour: earrings, a mix tape CD, a chrome vibrator. *Animal show* even here I thought. *Male bowerbird. Attracts female with gifts, the shinier the better.*

Instinctually, I looked for the Men's room, but then remembered who I was. I took a deep breath and pushed open the Ladies' door. There was a group of babes and butches standing in front of the long mirror over the sinks. I slipped into a stall, closed the door, and at the last second remembered to sit instead of stand.

"You gotta see Sarah Silverman," one of the women said at the mirror. "She's at the Improv. Caught her last night. One of her lines cracked me up; 'It's so cool to have a vagina. Like having a pool in your backyard. And it's heated.' "

"The beauty is in the booty."

"My girl has some junk in *her* trunk. One time after she fucked me with a strap-on, I told her I never had it so good. She said it was because of her big fat ass. When I asked what that had to do with it, she said, 'You can't drive a spike with a tack hammer!' "

They shrieked.

I ran out as fast as my heels could carry me.

"Oh, my," Suki said. "What happened? You look so pale."

"Women can be *ten times* raunchier than men! It was enough to make a crow blush."

"Ready to go?" she said.

We grabbed a cab and started kissing in the back seat. We burst into Suki's apartment, stumbling against each other, tugging clothes off. We fell onto the bed, then she pulled away going into the bathroom.

"Keep your panties on," she called. "I want you both soft—and hard!"

Early the next morning, Suki left for work dressed in a business suit and toting a briefcase. She leaned over the bed and pecked me on the cheek. "You're what every woman needs," she whispered in my ear.

"Whaa?" I asked groggily.

"A wife." She smiled and walked out the door.

I got up wincing, staggering, and clutching my head in pain from the multi-martini hangover. Looking at the mirror in the bright light of day the full impact of what I had done hit me. The wig was askew. What makeup left was a smeary mess. A furry eyelash drooped down onto my cheek. One-by-one, I pulled off the female adornments having an especially painful time plucking off the nails. *Shanghai Shimmer—my ass!* In the shower while lathering up there was no drag, the soap kept falling away against my smooth-shaven legs and sleek body. I stared. I remembered. I shook my head. *WHAT THE HELL WAS I THINKING?*

Stepping out of the bathroom, I reclaimed my maleness by grimacing, growling, and flexing my arms—reloading my *guns*—in front of the mirror. I punctuated the exhibition by pounding a fist up against a taut pec. Other motion caught my eye. I saw a mug of tea still steaming that Suki had set down on the bedside table. Alongside was a handwritten note: *Orlando, I salute your bravery! Always remember: "The soul has no gender." —Virginia Woolf*

That evening, I called Suki. "Hey, I want to thank you for the most enlightening night of my life."

"Glad you called. I talked about you today."

"WHAT! You gave your…"

"My lesbian girlfriends got after me at lunch, saying I should quit dicking around and go gay completely. So, I told them about you—not by name—just that I slept with a man last night. And you know what finally shut them up?"

"What?"

"I said that you eat pussy better than they do."

"Maybe I should wear a dress more often?"

"Yes, Orlando…cloak your manliness with feminine strength and refinements and you'll be well on your way to being a complete person."

After hanging up the phone, I took her note out of my pocket. I picked up a pen and drew a box around: *"The soul has no gender." —Virginia Woolf.* Across the top, I scribbled:

*THEOREM #6: INSIDE THE BOX.*

# 16

## "…I'm a Human Being."

*"Step inside, walk this way*
*You and me babe, hey, hey!"*

I was backstage at the Variety Arts Theater on 3rd Avenue in a Men's room—bent over puking into a sink while Def Leppard's *Pour Some Sugar on Me* boomed throughout the theater cueing my segment of *The Bid for Bachelors Charity Auction.* My nervous butterflies had turned into vampire bats that now wreaked havoc with my stomach.

The show's producer wearing a headphone and tapping a Palm Pilot dashed around backstage calling my name. I was last up in the procession of New York City's most eligible single guys, the headliner being *Cosmo's* Bachelor . The theater was packed with five hundred women thoroughly warmed up with juices flowing as they reveled in the turnabout of men being the objectified as the bachelors individually strolled on a long walk way thrusting out from the stage into the center of the audience. Even backstage the air carried a hopped-up, erotic charge.

*"Love is like a bomb, baby, c'mon get it on…*
*Demolition woman, can I be your man?"*

I stepped out of the Men's room. "Dude, you're up!" The producer grabbed my arm and led me to the curtain. He barked into his mike: "Go time!"

The Master of Ceremonies, the TV announcer for the New York Yankees, stood at a podium stage left wearing a crimson velour blazer topped with a red-and-white Santa Claus hat.

He yelled into the microphone, "AND NOW...WHAT YOU'VE ALL BEEN WAITING FOR...THE MAN WHO

NEEDS NO INTRO-DUCTION... GOTHAM'S OWN... BY WAY OF ALASKA...*COSMO'S* BACHELOR—MICHAEL *FOREVER WILD…*" My last name was drowned by a rising wall of high-pitched sound like a jet aircraft taking off.

*"...Take a bottle, shake it up..."*

I pawed frantically at the curtain, not finding the opening.

*"Break the bubble, break it up"*

Finally, I stumbled out on stage. I stood there blinking like a deer caught in hundreds of headlights. I gulped, reminding myself that courage is a form of fear turned around. The women jumped to their feet, screaming and dancing in place.

*"Pour some sugar on me*
*Ooh, in the name of love*
*Pour some sugar on me*
*C'mon fire me up"*

Palms sweating, legs trembling, I crept slowly down the runway.

*"Pour your sugar on me..."*

The M.C. called out dollar amounts. Auction paddles rose, and a phalanx of long, thin arms reached out to me from both sides of the cat walk. Interrupting the raucous reception were a few piercing wolf whistles and calls, including: "NICE ASS!" Reaching the end of the runway, I stopped—finally warming to the task.

*"I'm hot, sticky sweet*
*From my head to my feet yeah"*

The TV monitor flashed a text message number and e-mail address for viewers of the local cable station to place their bids at home.

*"You got the peaches, I got the cream"*

I took a deep breath and thought, *Ellen, you better be right...*

*"Do you take sugar?"*

I slowly lowered one arm at an angle below my waist and crossed it with the other arm.

*"One lump or two?"*

In one forward motion, I pulled off the tear-away pants and flung them out into the audience. There was a momentary, collective gasp—then the women's screams nearly raised the roof, seeing a kilt fall down over my bare legs.

Something wasn't right, felt imbalanced. I looked down. The white, fur-covered spooren, the ancient Scottish man purse fronting the kilt was entangled in its chains. A tall, gorgeous woman closest to the end of the runway reached up and yanked it down.

"Nice package!" I read from her lips amidst the wild uproar.

Gaining confidence, I gave her a grateful wink, turned, and walked back up the runway. Bidding paddles rose into the air and then swung, spanking me as I strutted by.

*"Take a bottle, shake it up*
*Break the bottle, break it up"*

I stopped halfway. *What the hell. I've been to the gym every day ...* I spun around. Feeling the love, and to give the bids a boost, my fists grabbed the Velcroed tuxedo jacket and shirt underneath and they too went flying through the air. I stood there wearing nothing but a forest green kilt, black leather combat boots, and a randy smile.

*"Pour some sugar on me*
*Ooh, in the name of love*
*Pour some sugar on me*
*C'mon fire me up"*

I turned and danced on down the stage. I stopped again in front of the curtain, dripping sweat from nerves and hot lights. With my back to the screaming horde, I spread my legs apart, cocked-out a kilt-clad left hip, and raised my right arm. My wrist twisted upward...

*"Yeah! Sugar me!"*

As the song ended, my index and pinkie finger flashed and held the sign for "Rock On."

A hot-pink thong soared as if in slow motion through the air, and I caught it on my little finger—swinging it around and around...

The lights went down.

The crowd went crazy.

The bids zoomed up.

Backstage, realizing what I had done and suddenly feeling ridiculous in front of the guys, I grabbed the end of the curtain and wrapped it around myself. I handed the thong to the waiting producer.

He grinned and pocketed the slight assemblage of strings. "You killed. This way," he said leading me to a computer station.

The house lights came on and the M.C. announced to the crowd that the winner was not in their midst, but that the top bid had come in via e-mail. "And who might this mystery woman be?" the M.C. inquired.

Backstage the producer tapped an e-mail back to the winner asking for her identity. I watched the computer screen closely. *Zelda Zephyr* appeared. The producer relayed her name over the headphone to the M.C.

He announced to the audience, "How about a big hand for Ms. Zelda Zephyr? Her winning bid was the highest of the evening, three-thousand dollars going to the United Way. For the Bachelors tonight…all told…ladies, whether here or out there in TV land, you raised forty-two thousand dollars for a very worthy cause! In this season of giving, Happy Holidays to one and all!"

After a production assistant asked for Zelda Zephyr's credit card information, I stepped up to the computer and personally thanked her for the donation via instant messaging. We conversed, setting the night, place, and time to meet. She said she hoped I had a large car. When I responded: *???*, she explained: "I have a bit of a weight problem. And many years and grey hairs on you. Maybe you should go with the next bidder down, one of those young chicky-babes. I'll understand..."

My hands hovered above the keyboard for a moment, then I quickly rapped: "No, no. See you Friday @ eight."

Friday night I rolled across Manhattan in the back seat of a white limo, a prime requirement for any Bid-for-Bachelors' dinner date and hopefully a roomy, expansive solution to Zelda Zephyr's aforementioned physical *largess.* Surrounded by luxury and glancing out the one-way black tinted windows I swallowed hard, feeling exhilaration tinged with sadness. This was not my first time riding inside a comfort carriage. After going limo-less my whole unglamorous life, it was my second time rolling in such an extravagant ride in two weeks.

Feeling extremely horny after the aborted date with Miss Memphis, I impulsively accepted an offer from the female CEO of a big company in Canada and *Cosmo* invitee. I called her on a Friday afternoon—then took a forty-minute hopper flight up to Toronto. She was waiting in a big stretch limo which she instructed the chauffeur to just drive around town. She pressed a button and a maple-burled panel sealed us off inside our own private, padded boudoir.

She was like a barracuda—long, smooth, and all about a predator's aggressive forward motion. I was her chew toy. She had my clothes off within minutes; she was naked under a fur coat and we fucked on the wide seat, down on the thick carpet, and seemingly across the padded ceiling—while looking out upon the normal everyday world.

"Claire, you *sure* no one can see us?" I asked repeatedly as we bounced and tussled, building up a sweat with snow banks piled outside in wintry Toronto, and people in surrounding cars slowing to stare with the celebrity-crazed cultural curiosity that a white limousine with dark windows automatically causes.

With the limo at a dead stop at a red light and Claire and I furiously pouring the coal in back, I glanced out to see an innocent-looking boy with a buzz cut and thick glasses (reminding me of my past self) roll down his window and stare open-mouthed. I felt totally exposed and lost my, *ahem,* concentration—recoiling from a sudden attack of Catholic school induced guilt-and-shame.

Further on, in the depths of downtown, the driver hit a deep pothole and Claire and I abruptly uncoupled and were thrown back on opposite sides of the padded pleasure dome. Arms outstretched, panting madly, me once-again Catholic-conflicted and about to call the whole thing off, but Claire was so damned divinely curvy, silky, nectar-sweet, to say nothing of being voraciously insatiable that I eagerly answered the call of the wild once again with every cell gleefully singing *A-ROOOOOO!!*

When we did take a break from shagging, charging into a raw bar to eat oysters (what else!) spattered with Tabasco sauce and chased with shots of chilled vodka, Claire said that she was married. And the only way, realistically, for a marriage to last was to acknowledge our animal natures and give them their due. She and her husband had both agreed to issue each other two free passes a year to act on their lust for other people without it harming the marriage.

"We have holidays for everything else," she said. "We need a couple breaks to honor our animal natures and then come back refreshed to the same partner. So unnecessary all this trauma and drama over cheating," she shrugged, "when once in a while we just need to feed our animal side and the excitement and joy that it brings."

With the present-time limousine slowing down near Zelda Zephyr's address, even though impeccably dressed now in a tailored suit and silk tie, I struggled to quick-kill a raging memory erection. But I couldn't resist scratching myself high and low as all of my body hair, shaven at Suki's, was now in the early tortuous stage of growing back in. *Beneath the sartorial splendor lurks the hirsute beast,* I thought—clawing away.

Other than the constant itch, I felt good about myself now and looked forward to a relaxed, pleasant evening with the stolid Ms. Zephyr. Passivity, after so much non-stop *Cosmo* girl calamity would be a welcomed relief.

The driver stopped. I pressed Zelda's door buzzer with one hand—while getting in one more quick dig with the other, below the belt, to tame the bristly irritation. The door opened and my mouth fell open. "What the—*SKYLER?*"

"Yeah, yeah, I needed the tax write-off. Good cause, United Way. Although, you took me a bit past my limit after you tore your pants off."

"I don't believe—WOW. You look fantastic." I squinted. "I thought you said you were fat and…"

She led me to an elevator. "Just testing you."

"Did you think I wouldn't show?"

"Wasn't sure," she said, her eyes narrowing as the elevator door closed. "After walking in on your bar brawl in London, I thought you liked 'em fresh from the cradle. Goldilocks was all over you. How old was she, *sixteen?*"

"I was set up," I said, touching my still tender eye.

She looked me up and down, then arched an eyebrow. "And what, no kilt?"

I hung my head.

"What got into you? You turned into a Chippendale's dancer."

"My friend, Ellen, gave me the idea of the tear-away clothes. The kilt was my doing. And Ellen said she would donate $5,000.00 anonymously, or double it if I went the full monty."

"Well, you put on quite a show. You know," she said, her attitude softening somewhat. "There's something I've always wondered…"

"Shoot."

"What is worn under a kilt?"

"Nothing's *worn*, lass—everything is in perfect working order."

Stepping out of the elevator, she rolled her eyes, but couldn't help laughing.

After entering her apartment, I stopped abruptly, staring at hundreds of books on pine-wood shelves lining the walls from floor-to-ceiling.

"Didn't have a chance to go to college," she shrugged. "So, I'm educating myself."

I walked toward a shelf. "You know how paper books are certain to be replaced by digital reading devices, like the Kindle?"

"Yeah."

"Well, I don't buy it. Besides the portability and aesthetic properties," I paused to pluck a hardcover off the shelf, "books are so sensual." I cracked open the volume, raised it to my face, and sniffed deeply. "I love the way they smell. I can tell if a book is going to be a good read by how it smells."

"You're an animal."

As she turned to get her purse, I noticed my Alaska book face down on a side table by the couch. Walking by the book without looking she rapped a curled finger on the dust-jacket photo. "If I see that picture one more time, I'll puke. It's *everywhere*—all over town."

"I know. It's sickening."

"Let's go. Can't wait to see *The Hunk of the Month*or is it *The Playboy of the Western World* in action. Besides, we only got to talk in bits and pieces at thirty thousand feet and you said you wanted a sounding board, someone to share some ideas with. That I am…at your service." She hooked her arm though mine, staring straight ahead. "And seemingly the only female on earth not at all swayed by your rugged good looks."

The uniformed driver held open the limo door. Once underway, Skyler ran her hands over the crushed-velvet, purple seat and ceiling. "Feels like we're in a womb."

I blushed, flashing back to insatiable CEO Claire. *No, she can't know* ... I poured two flutes of champagne.

We sat back, sipping the bubbly. I recovered somewhat, saying, "That monk had it right..."

"Who?"

"Dom Pérignon, the Benedictine monk who invented champagne. At first sip, he said it was *like drinking stars.*"

"Nice." She touched her glass to mine and a crystal tone rang through the padded carriage.

We chatted idly about movies for a few minutes. When I asked who Skyler's favorite actress was, she responded immediately.

"Mae West, the original ball-breaker. She took no prisoners and not a bit of guff. My favorite scene was inside Mae's lavish mansion when she lined up a dozen statuesque studs in bath towels barely held together; the *Cosmo Bachelors* of their day. A young Tom Selleck was in the line-up, one of his first roles. Finally, before picking one to send up to her boudoir, she says..." Skyler slid down onto her knees, placed a hand on a swaying hip and in a sultry voice murmured, "All right boys—get out yah *résumés.*"

"That was so *her!*" I said laughing. "One more, do one more—please."

Just then the limo glided to a stop in front of the restaurant. As the chauffeur opened the door, I hopped out, sneaking in another scratch. Like a movie star playing the moment for all it was worth, Skyler emerged slowly—stiletto heel stabbing the air and a creamy white thigh flashing through her slit black skirt. Shoulders back, chest out, she glanced at the driver, then at me.

Her hands lifted to cradle our chins, "I only like two kinds of men: Foreign and Domestic."

We entered the restaurant laughing. Over dinner, Skyler asked about my *Cosmo* dates so far. I told her about my latest encounters with the samba dancer and the southern belle.

She seemed skeptical that anything of value could result from my run as a *Cosmo* Bachelor.

"Now that you're not teaching anymore, what do you do to make a living?"

"I'm working on my second book."

"A sequel on Alaska and the whales?"

"No, a field study of *Cosmo* women."

Both eyebrows arched. "And how many women have written to you?"

"Thousands. It's em…"

"Michael, you bastard! You're nothing but a fucking phony. Hiding your real motives under the guise of some scientific *research* when you're nothing more than a pussy hound, just like all the rest. GROW UP!" She flung her napkin down into her soup, her other hand twitching around for a projectile.

"No, no, that's not my inten…"

I tried to defend myself, but she latched onto the protruding corner of a thin paperback sticking out of her purse and whipped it through the air. It struck me dead-center between the eyes. I heard the restaurant door swing open and Skyler's throaty roar: *"TAXI!"*

My head fell forward. Feeling all eyes in the restaurant upon me, I scooped up the book, *A Doll's House* by Henrik Ibsen, and pretended to read. A highlighted sentence leapt off the page: *Nora said, "Before everything else I'm a human being."*

I reached under the table and scratched myself raw.

# 17

## "Diogenes Roamed the Earth…"

At the low point of my Bachelor journey, feeling like shit for upsetting someone as classy and cultured as Skyler, I couldn't concentrate on anything but my remorse for having ended our date, once again, so badly. I moped around all day and finally that night I fired up the laptop to write:

*Dear Ms. Zephyr (wherever you are),*

*Thanks for the extended loan of Ibsen's brilliant A Doll's House. The book hit me right between the eyes. Any other volumes in your lending library? Soft-cover, please.*

*Seriously, as you are well aware I have a lot to learn, and being male can only wrap my brain around one pearl of wisdom at a time, please. Thanks.*

*Your Friend and (someday) Fellow Human Being,*
*Klondike Mike*

I hit *Send* and got up and fed Charlie. I was gathering together my dirty clothes to go out and do long-neglected laundry when I heard the electronic tone of incoming mail. Shocked—it was Skyler; I dropped into the chair and read:

*Dear Klondike Mike,*

THE MOTHER LODE: *Simone de Beauvoir's The Second Sex; Doris Lessing's The Golden Notebook;*

*Carol Tavris' The Mismeasure of Woman; Fay Weldon's The Life and Loves of a She-Devil; Clarissa Pinkola Estes' Women Who Run with the Wolves; Camille Paglia's Sexual Personae; Naomi Wolf's The Beauty Myth; Eve Ensler's The Vagina Monologues. That should hold you for a while.*

*—Z.Z.*

*PS: The Greek philosopher Diogenes roamed the earth carrying a lamp during the daytime looking for one honest man. He finally gave up. Maybe, just maybe, he failed to open the October issue of Cosmopolitan.*

# 18

# Wind Through Her Hair

Early Saturday morning, I started in on a top-to-bottom cleaning of my apartment. After removing deep layers of dust and grime, I was thinking of brightening up the place with a Christmas tree when the phone rang. Hearing Ellen's voice on the answering machine, I picked up.

"Hey," I said, "what's new?"

"I've decided to leave New York. I'm off to Africa to do an anthro-archaeological dig in a remote archipelago off the coast of Madagascar. Want to come?"

"What!"

"It's something I've been planning for a long time. I didn't want to tell you about it until a product I invented took off."

"You invented a product? Wow. What is it?"

"You know those inflated exercise balls they have at the gym that you lie back on and do sit-up crunches because the ball supports you so well and isolates the abs?"

"Yeah."

"Well, one day after stomach-crunching, I was sitting on the ball mindlessly bouncing up and down and I got a little turned on."

"Why am I not surprised?" I said.

"While I was bouncing with the motion so similar to sex, I thought why not ramp it up and screw in dildos on the top of the ball? After many trial runs using myself as the tester, of course, I got the shapes and lengths of the dildos—pliable clear rubber, washable, and in an assortment of colors—just right. The double dildo, named the *Dick Dock*, bends the very time-space continuum, sending a woman out of this world. The main shaft is irregularly ribbed and there's a curved tapered prong in front to simultaneously hit the clit. And you know how I said that I would think about getting married if I ever met a guy with two cocks?"

"Yeah."

"Well, you simply turn around on the dildo and the curved prong goes up the ass as well. And the woman is in total control. The harder you bounce, the deeper the satisfaction. The more you put out, the more you get in. Hey—you know, that's not a bad sales slogan. And since the ball is such a launching pad, I gave each dildo a futuristic or fantasy film title or character name—tweaked erotically, of course. There's Deep Space 9, Starship Uranus, Whore of the Rings, Austin Prowler, Boldfinger, Darth Madeher, Hand Solo, and Jabba the Muff. Anyway, a couple demonstrations on TV: the *Spice* channel and Howard Sperm raving about it on *SIRIUS* Satellite Radio and the dildo ball took off like a rocket. We're moving 100,000 units a week, worldwide. Check out the website, Have-a-Ball.org. *Org* for orgasm."

"Ellen," I said, my mind's eye following the bouncing ball, "you never cease to amaze..." I felt the erotic images downloading directly to my hard drive. "Umm, was there some mention earlier of an expedition?"

"Yeah, that was my point. It's all privately funded now by my own, *Have-a-Ball* cash flow. Don't have to ask Daddy to prematurely open up a trust fund."

"Tell me more—about the expedition."

"There are several marine mammal species that haven't been fully studied, plus there's a rumor of a living aquatic dinosaur that the island natives swear they've seen. Find that, Morani, and you're famous for all time! The archipelago is out in the Indian Ocean—coelacanth country. If a fish that was extinct for eighty million years recently turned up, just think what else is swimming around down there."

"Well, this is quite a surprise. I mean it's great, but when would we leave?"

"In a little over a week, just before the new year. I'm starting to cargo box all my tools and instruments as we speak."

"Can I have a couple days to decide?"

"Sure. Besides the work, I thought it would be a retreat back to that island isolation you enjoyed so much up in Alaska. And I can't think of a better man to have with me. You and I could handle the close quarters and primitive conditions without tearing each other apart."

"But what about being bored? Could Ellen Klein actually be monogamous for that long, or are you bringing Dick Dock or Darth Madeher along?"

"No, no. You know me, I prefer the real thing. We can work in a native boy or two for me, and some jungle fever for you."

I shook my head. "You're incorrigible."

"I've been reading Erica Jong. Great writer and sexual pioneer. She wrote, 'Monogamy is impossible among interesting people.' "

"There's nothing dull about you, that's for sure. Ellen—thanks. I'm honored that you would invite me."

"Just say yes."

"Maybe. I'll call you soon."

"Hey, before you go. Good job at the Bachelors' Auction, but I kept waiting for you to whip off the kilt too."

"No way. I don't even know how I did what I did."

"Well, I paid United Way the 5K—only if you had showed the girls *The North Pole,* I would have doubled it!"

"Bye, Ellen."

"OK. But holla back soon with your decision."

Stunned, I flopped onto the couch. *Well, I guess no need for a Christmas tree...* Still aroused, I glanced over at the empty corner of the apartment and to brighten up the place, I mentally substituted a rotund, rubber-spiked ball with a half-dozen naked fem-bots bouncing together up and down—lit up brighter than any tree with their nipples flashing red and green and anatomically correct pubic strips glittering like Yuletide tinsel.

To break the spell, I jumped up and on impulse phoned Skyler. She was home. I thanked her for the e-mail. She said she had just been in Paris and checked her e-mail at the airport before flying home. I asked if she wanted to go to the zoo in Central Park, to just hang out together for a few hours?

"Why not? I haven't been to the zoo since I was a little girl."

"Great. Meet you at the entrance in, say, an hour?"

"Fine. See you then."

No sooner did I hang up the phone when my apartment intercom buzzer rang from the street below.

"Yes?" I said, wondering who it could be.

"Is this Michael?"

I didn't recognize the voice. It was female, a bit older, with raw undertones.

"Uh, no—I'm his brother." I winced after the lie. "Who is this?"

"Deloris. I'm the prisoner who wrote and said she was getting out soon," she paused to emit a gruesome laugh, "and needs a boyfriend *bad*. Is he around?"

"No, he's, um—away on a trip."

"I understand. He doesn't want to see me, considering where I've been and all."

"No, no. Hey, sometimes bad things happen to good people."

"Thank you. You sound nice."

"No! I'm the bad brother." I pressed the button again. "Um, I make babies cry just walking by." I cringed. "By the way, what were you in for?"

"Walked in on my husband screwing my best friend. Blew him away with a shotgun. Pled temporary insanity. Jury bought it. Got Man One, but I'm out early on good behavior. You know," her voice dropped even lower, "it's bad boys that really float my boat."

"I gotta go! Bye." My finger flew off the intercom button as if electrocuted.

I doubled-bolted the door and waited as long as possible before throwing on warm clothes. I flipped the collar up on the navy pea coat and tugged the brim of a Yankees baseball cap down low over my face. I opened the bedroom window and worked my way down the fire escape in case the horny ex-con was still lurking out front.

Skyler was waiting at the zoo entrance, glancing at her watch.

"Sorry I'm late. Couldn't find a cab," I said, panting from running. Doubled-over to catch my breath, I looked over my shoulder down the street.

"You OK? Is someone chasing you?"

I explained about Deloris. Skyler shook her head. "I knew your life was crazy, but it's gone way past that into the surreal. My God, Michael…be careful!"

We entered the zoo. As we walked, talked, and stopped to view the animals, I began to relax and enjoy the way Skyler made me feel. I told her that it was wonderful having a woman for a friend.

"You say that like you're the first man to land on the moon. It *is* possible, you know for men and women to just be friends, if men would think with an organ other than their dicks."

"I know," I paused and smiled, "but it's difficult. Robin Williams says: 'A man has two heads and only enough blood to run one at a time.' "

We went into the Avian Conservation Center where injured raptors were rehabilitated for release back into the wild. As I talked with the director, Skyler looked at the line-up of perched owls, hawks, and falcons. Seeing them close up, I saw her admire their beauty. Their feathers were perfectly fitted. Their oversized, prismatic eyes flashed like jewels.

With the director, I turned a corner into another room.

A few minutes later I called, "Skyler, in here."

She entered the room and gasped. Standing on my leather-sleeved arm was a bald eagle nearly three-feet tall and flapping seven-feet of wings. The eagle's eyes locked onto Skyler's as its colossal wings oared the air, streaming wind through her hair. Skyler's normally guarded face was wide-open and childlike; her eyes filled with wonder.

The director explained that the eagle was there because of being shot by a hunter in Alaska. It was a felony and a federal offense to try to kill the US national symbol, but there were no witnesses to the crime. A bush pilot spotted the eagle hopping around dragging a broken wing. The pilot netted the bird and had it flown to the Avian Conservation Center for the best medical care. Buckshot had also grazed his heart. Now, miraculously, after three operations, *Chak*, the Chaktalnulth Native word for eagle, was ready to be returned to the wild.

As Skyler and I left the Avian Center, I told her that in the wild eagles live about twenty-five years and mate for life, a rarity in the animal kingdom.

"How do they choose each other?" she asked.

"It's actually quite incredible. They conduct their courtship by flying full speed at one another, thousands of feet up in the air in a game of aerial chicken. Then, in the last few feet of space before colliding head-on, the male flips over onto his back and extends his legs, talons open. If the female likes what she sees, she grabs hold; they lock talons and tumble—cart wheeling together over and over one another in a freefall down to the ocean. A few feet above the sea, they unlock talons—then climb back up to do it again and again."

"Gives new meaning to being swept off your feet."

"Yeah, makes dinner and a movie seem kinda tame." We smiled.

"Then they mate and build a nest together," I continued. "Eagles use the same nest year after year. It keeps growing and growing and some get as big as a condo. In the spring in Alaska, I watched the mated pairs fly wing-to-wing through the forest gathering materials to repair their nests damaged by the winter storms."

I explained that I try not to be anthropomorphic about animals, but *romantic* is the word I'd use to describe them when nesting. "The male tries to impress his lady with some exotic present to spruce up their home. They're very opportunistic and will beach comb for all sorts of found objects—anything to help hold the nest together. Because fishing boats throw a lot of things overboard that wash up on shore, the nests are always full of surprises."

I told her, "One day, when the parents were out fishing, I climbed up to a nest to photograph the chicks. When I got up there, I almost fell out of the tree. Spread out in the bottom of the nest was the front page of *The New York Times.* Home delivery, but without the blue plastic wrapper. It was spread out as a diaper for the chicks. They normally use moss. After that lofty journalism was soiled, Mama Eagle kicked it out and there was the newspaper a few days later recycling directly back into the forest floor."

"A couple weeks after that in another nest, I saw a long white object woven down vertically through the sticks. It looked man-made, elastic, like it had been stretched. Couldn't figure out what it was until I got closer. It was a ladies' bikini top. Worked wonders on holding an eagle nest together, but it sure wreaked havoc with a lonely hermit's heart."

Skyler stopped walking. She looked at me in a different way, with warmth and softness. A mischievous grin spread across her face. "And you probably stole that bra and took it back to your cabin to play with."

I laughed. "Yeah, I thought about it."

We continued walking. "What's most impressive is their eyes," she said. "When I looked into Chak's inside the aviary, it's as if he stared right into my soul."

I nodded. "The Chaktalnulth tribe feels that *Eagle* is the messenger between the natural and supernatural world and that they can see into the future. An eagle's eyesight is one of nature's miracles. From a distance of two miles away, a bald eagle can spot a tiny, eight-inch fish on the surface of the sea."

"If we were sitting inside a stadium, high-up in the nosebleed seats and a bald eagle was up there with us, from that height we would see the field as a green rectangle. The eagle would see the green rectangle and after blinking and refocusing it would see *every blade of grass* in the field. They have what's called High Definition Eyesight."

As we strolled past other animals in their habitat enclosures, I explained the mating habits of each. "When female lions are in heat, the male will mate with her hundreds of times, biting the lioness by the scruff of her neck or the ear to hold on."

"Lovely."

"He does it around the clock, hour after hour, day after day for two weeks straight. He's obsessed—doesn't eat or sleep and loses a third of his body weight. And see that big silverback male gorilla over there? A harem of ten to twelve females keeps him thumping his chest."

We walked closer to the gorilla enclosure. "Amazing," she said, "how human their hands and facial expressions are!"

"Ninety-eight point six percent of their DNA is identical to humans." As we turned and strolled away, I continued, "Being so closely related to apes, social biologists say that so much of what we do is artificial and that's what causes pain and gets us in trouble. Our feet aren't meant to be in shoes eight hours a day or our bodies to sit sedentary at desks and in front of televisions and computers to the detriment of our health. And like the great apes, our nearest kin, we are not meant to be monogamous. That we belong, like them, in troops of shared sexuality."

"So, it's really us in the cages, not the animals," she commented.

"So true, the greatest anthropologist wasn't Margaret Mead, it was her ex-husband, Gregory Bateson. He nailed it, saying: 'The major problems in the world exist because of the differences between the way nature works and the way man thinks.' "

"Besides eagles, are there *any* species that are faithful?"

I thought about it. "Wolves, beavers…but that's about it. And most birds are cheaters supreme, especially the females—taking on all comers, pardon the pun. They do it to make absolutely certain they're fertilized during their brief estrus. We used to think that ducks and geese were paragons of virtue, faithful for life, but recent DNA tests of female eggs showed they were actually fertilized by multiple partners. And dolphins and whales—*fahgetaboutit.* They specialize in ménages à trois; two males often mate with one female. Afterwards, the permanent family structure becomes matriarchal. Same with the elephants—over there," I pointed. "After breeding the males rogue off, leaving the females to raise the young."

"Sounds all too familiar," she muttered.

We stopped in front of the penguin display.

"Oh, they are *sooo* cute!" she said.

"And major players, too."

"No. Don't tell me. All right," she sighed. "Do."

"Well, I don't know which one she is..." I said, scanning the penguins. "But the zoo keepers call one of the penguins, *Paris Hilton.* It seems that when she sashays past the married males, they burst out of their burrows, jump her bones, and then bring back a shiny stalk of grass or a wild flower to their wives, like: 'Honey, I was just out looking for a present for you!' "

Skyler groaned.

"Hey, men are people, too."

"Sometimes."

"Speaking of presents..." I stopped, looking around. "This way."

We walked into the Tropical Bird House, removing our coats in the heated-up habitat. "Here," I said. "Look at this."

A Satin Bowerbird hopped back and forth across the forest floor in front of a small wedding bower, composed of twigs and complete with a proscenium arch. Leading to the bower was a walkway outlined with small objects—berries, feathers, flowers, a Bic pen cap, and pebbles.

"And here," I said, leading Skyler closer to the guard-railing above the bower. "See how the little house is painted in places, dark blue?"

"Yes. But how?"

"The male Bowerbird did that, too. He colors his saliva with compounds such as charcoal and leaf juices. Notice how the walls and most of his objects, like him, are either blue or black?

"Yes. Color-coordinated," she said, in awe.

"Male Bowerbirds tend to collect things that match their own plumage colors. And he's now waiting for a female Bowerbird to come by. If she likes his property and display, they mate."

Skyler stepped back. "The comparison to human behavior is uncanny—the male attracts a mate with real estate and offers *colored rocks*." She paused, letting it all soak in. "After they mate, does the female move in with him?"

"No. After mating, she goes off and nests by herself. And the male continues advertising for babes at his bower, mating with as many females as he can attract."

Skyler leaned back over the railing and gave the bird a flinty look. "I'm giving him a name."

"What?"

"Hugh Hefner."

I smiled. "Only his girls live at the Mansion."

"Oh, look!"

On the other side of the walkway enclosed in a large canopy of fine-mesh net, hummingbirds zinged back and forth, their iridescent colors flashing like errant rainbows.

"They're my favorites!" Skyler exclaimed, her head lifting and turning as she followed their mesmerizing flight paths. "The first poem I ever memorized in school was about a hummingbird by Emily Dickinson."

"Bet I know what it is."

"What? No way that Mister Macho knows Emily Dickinson. You're putting me on."

"No, I'm not."

"Say it, then."

I hesitated. "Only if you recite it with me."

Together, we began without missing a beat:

*A Route of Evanescence*

*With a revolving Wheel*
*A Resonance of Emerald*
*A Rush of Cochineal*
*And every Blossom on the Bush*
*Adjusts its tumbled Head*
*The mail from Tunis, probably*
*An easy Morning's Ride.*

Skyler jumped up and down with glee.

"OK," she said, re-composing herself, "how do they do it while in flight?"

"The males are lek breeders. They all gather at mating sites called *leks*. Each male stakes out a small territory, a perch on a flower or vine. He sings his squeaky tune and fluffs up his tiny feathers. Females enter the lek and choose a male to mate with."

Skyler sighed. "I see that on Friday night in every bar I walk into."

We moved on to The Rare Plants Conservatory and paused to take in a riot of forms and colors. "Native Americans feel that flowers are the most highly evolved forms of life," I said, "for they give beauty without asking anything in return."

She was astonished. "I've never seen plants like this. It's like they are sentient—thinking or breathing!"

I looked at her and smiled. "In their own right, they are. Some can see..."

We walked over to a dark box penetrated only by a pinhole of light. "That shoot in there creeps out toward the smallest light source. They can count... Here, the Venus Flytrap. It closes up tight when its trigger hair is touched not once, but twice."

I demonstrated by reaching out and stroking a bristly hair with my finger. "They communicate with one another chemically and can estimate time with extraordinary precision."

"Smarty plants," she said.

We stopped in front of a flowering vine. "This one grows high in the forest canopy of South America, hanging down like that, half-a-dozen blooms in a row."

"They look like little buckets."

"You got it. The *Bucket Flower*. The front of the blossom—here, look closer. The front is made up of two small legs. When the legs open, small glands secrete nectar that fills the bucket to a depth of a quarter-inch. The scent of the nectar is so alluring that it drives the boys wild. A special bee, the Furry Carpenter arrives..."

"Do they wear little tool belts?" she teased.

I grinned, then took a moment to chase away the mental image of Shareen the butt model encased in said leather holster. "As they swarm, excited by the sweet scent, one bee falls or is knocked into the bucket. Drenched in nectar, he's too heavy to fly out and the flower walls are too slippery to climb. He enters a side tunnel here. It's a very tight fit where the flower is then pollinated. It's really a symbiotic re…"

"Stop it. I'm getting turned on."

"Well, then, we won't go into orchids..."

"What's this one?" she asked, gravitating toward a large-leafed plant off to the side standing alone. We both stopped before it admiring its vibrant foliage.

"Ah, *Acacia Romanticus,* better known as The Flame of the Forest. Incredible plant. Grows from the tropics all the way up to Alaska and has a legend attached. It seems that two young natives in Alaska were attracted to one another, but the male was too shy to speak his true feelings for the female. While walking together one full moon night, he was about to finally speak from his heart. But on the edge of the forest near a glacier, a big chunk of ice broke free and toppled over crushing them both. On the spot where the couple died this plant grew. As if to commemorate their unrequited love, it puts forth a brilliant red bloom, but for only one night a year."

I leaned over to stare closely at the tight bud. "With the New Year what, a few days away…doesn't look like it's going to make it this year."

After a late lunch at a Central Park café, I walked Skyler home and returned to my apartment feeling totally refreshed and rejuvenated. I opened the laptop and wrote:

*THEOREM #7: BACK TO NATURE*

It was great to get away for a few hours—back to the rich and balanced reality of flora and fauna. Thank goodness for Central Park. It is the lush green heart of, at times, a very harsh city. Couple things I thought about today... Just before he died, Einstein was working on the Theory of the Unified Field; he discovered that chlorophyll and human blood only differ by one atom.

Nature *is* human nature. Saw it in the plants today—how similar we are with our physical equipment and techniques of pollination/insemination—even the word, "orchid" means "testicle" (from the slope of its root) yet, with plants, even though it's all laid out naked in the open in balls-out or nectar-glistening displays before us, there's nothing shameful about it.

(What was that Mark Twain quote—"Nature knows no indecencies, man invents them.") Yet, unlike a bee, when a human male shows the same natural attraction to or appreciation for the female form it's "disgusting!"—the very word used by a young woman being ogled, not aggressive or grossly, but in amazed appreciation by a group of Italian boys coming out of the zoo (exchange students, their teacher said).

Accustomed to a coy smile or a witty toss of the shuttlecock back over the net at home in Rome, the boys here looked puzzled and hurt by the female's verbal slam. (Of course, the woman had on a miniskirt nearly up to her coochie and her coat open to a show of cleavage rivaling the Grand Canyon.)

To turn off the sex drive in a man is like the bee saying no to the flowers! It's where Life itself begins. (Heard Johnny O'Reilly, the septuagenarian stud from the gym, in my ear often today, saying that lust is the fuel that drives the engine of the universe.) Certainly saw that in action today in the zoo garden; I didn't see that at all in the urban jungle. Or I did see that, but it was shot down and denigrated as being *dirty*.

And the disconnect goes far beyond sex. I think we humans are too smart for our own good—turning our backs on nature (outside and in) and destroying the environment and ourselves in the process. No other animal, except man, fouls its own nest. If the first definition of intelligence is living in healthy harmony with your world, animals have a lot to teach us. If intelligence can be defined as the ability to solve problems, plants have much to share.

On the personal side—it was wonderful today being with Skyler, a true female friend. It's like having a *spy* now in the House of Femme. Note to self: Next time ask her what women really want in a man.

Read somewhere that when Yoko Ono first met John Lennon, she walked up and said one word to him: "Breathe." I was so relaxed, so myself with Skyler that throughout the day, amidst all our talking and walking, underneath it all I was conscious of the unconscious. I could feel myself breathing deeply and savoring each and every sip.

# 19

# Knot to Be Denied

Monday morning I headed over to Mission Control knowing that Rathbone and the TAs were away teaching at the university. I wanted to be alone. Entering the den, seeing the mountains of mail, women's pictures pinned up on the walls, lingerie and gifts scattered about, I still couldn't accept that this was all for me. *No, not really me—the Idea or Ideal of me.*

I randomly pulled out a few letters from the tall stacks and read:

> *"I want to share a little of my life as a jockey with you. It's the thrill of breaking from the gates, one with a finely-honed, pulsating mass of energy and muscle. That first explosion of energy is often the difference between getting the optimum position to set up for that all important win or losing the race in one fell swoop, knowing how much animal you have under you, how to get that little bit of extra at the end—the finish and of course the win. Nothing has meant more to me than my riding."*
> *—Caroline, South Carolina*

> *"…I decided to upgrade my violin. Within five minutes of first picking it up, I knew it was the one I was going to buy. It is very shiny, reddish-brown with muted golden brown trimmings. It was built in 1990 with no previous owners by a relatively unknown Polish maker named Mroz. It is a very chauvinistic business. Had it been Asian, it would have been a third less in cost, if German or American, three times as much, if Italian, four times*

*again. Strads go for millions. I got mine from a dealer I work with. I trust him implicitly. I had never before been interested in a brand-new instrument, but now I really like the idea of being the one to break it in. I use strings of silver. The sound is so bright, clear, and very even."*
*—Amie, Illinois*

*"... Our phone book is one-page long. Bears plod past our homes and a moose stuck its head in my bedroom window. We have more aircraft than cars. The library is the size of a garage and the post office doesn't have any mail trucks for there are no paved roads... It's the age-old problem: single women in a town full of men. The only obstacle to really enjoying Alaska the way I would love to is my sex. I am a single woman. Not a big deal to me, but the honest men say I can't go fishing or hiking with them or learn about whatever nature experiences they're doing because their wives will get jealous and so they carefully avoid contact with me. It's so much easier for a male to travel alone. People say he's looking for adventure, but when a female goes out to seek adventure, people say she's looking for trouble..."*
*—Sandra, Alaska*

*"Did you know that Jack Kerouac's manuscripts and papers are stored at The New York City Library? I'm writing a book about Kerouac's attitudes toward sex and religion. With all you must be going through, thought you might like this J.K. passage: 'What pleasures of the flesh! I want to start living again, no holds barred. As with Jinny last summer, a loving, vast, moist, softly undulating little fold—starry, lip-like, mound-like—a kind of eternity to its formless vastness. This is what all men want... Is this not the point of life? The cathedral, the pillars aspire only to this goal—let's admit it for God's sake... Why is everybody continually building moral laws as though we didn't have enough of them already to burden us with guilt.*

*No more sins and guilt, no more need for sins, no more guilt for not being guilty! Nothing but all things, frankly understood at last, rising from sexual energy outward to all human communications and situations. Let's just say "the hell with it" and become really creative at last... free, basking, wandering, idly stopping here and there, tasting, enjoying. Animals at last after the great interruption of ephemeral civilization... All things, all things must tend again to the garden of things.' "*
*—Erica, New York City*

I reached for pen and paper and scribbled:

*THEOREM # 8: KNOT TO BE DENIED*

The spirit, wisdom, and inner-wealth of women are staggering! Each woman is a lush garden unto herself full of beauty, knowledge, and inspiration. I'm now struggling with even the thought of getting married. Is there really just THE One, a "SUM-ONE" for everyone? Marriage presumes that one person can be everything to you and satisfy all of your needs and curiosities about this vast life forever. If married and Caroline, Amie, Sandra or Erica walk by, since I'm in marital "lock-down" I should shut my soul and look away. From the possessive wife's point of view, a husband shouldn't take the slightest chance or open the door at all to the possibility of falling in love with another woman. But is that any way to live while trying to be a lifelong learner? Act deaf, dumb, and blind to half the population of the planet? Be robbed of incredible insights from different perspectives? Live behind bars of possessiveness with the lock made of fear? If there are other, advanced civilizations in outer space, I sense that with them monogamy and jealousy are passé. Love by its very nature defies limitation. Why can't a man love more than one woman at the same time? We demonstrate every day that we have the capacity to love more than one parent, child, or pet equally. Why can't we have more than one "significant other"? It just doesn't seem natural or right for a man to lose the varied riches and valuable lessons from the incredible wealth of women.

# 20

# Sugar Shock

**Lorelai Logan**

**Species Name:** *Lorelai Loliti*

**Habitat & Range:** From trailer parks to the finest universities.

**Identifying Characteristics:** A morning glory bursting into bloom.

**Best Known For:** Pollination with a seasoned honeybee.

The next day I visited Ellen. She talked in detail about the Africa expedition; we poured over maps and thoroughly examined the distant logistics. For some unknown reason, I was still hesitant about going. That night, as if providing further impetus for persuasion, she personally gave me a full and varied demonstration of the bouncing dildo globe. A new sales option: her Have-a-Ball as a world globe, "so you can learn geography while sexercising."

While she was riding high and hot above the Arctic regions, I turned down her breathy request to make a detailed mold of my *North Pole* as an additional demarcation to her product line. She said she would gladly keep springing up and down in any position or over any country I desired for the solid hour it took for the latex to mold itself completely to my modeling member. Despite the opportunity to become a permanent fixture atop the world and repeated pleadings, Michael Polo declined.

The following morning, I borrowed Ellen's car and drove to Columbia University. Rathbone had called and left a message that he wanted to see me. From ingrained habit, I was about to park in the faculty section, but swerved at the last second into a visitor's spot. I entered the Science building and trod the familiar path to Dean Rathbone's office.

"Professor Mackenzie," Rathbone's secretary said. "You've got mail!" she giggled, and pointed to two canvas mail bags propped against the wall like two gray pillars. I could barely lift them off the ground.

"Ah, Michael, come in," said Rathbone in the open doorway to his office. He laughed, seeing me still eyeing the mail sacks with disbelief.

"Amazing how they find you," Rathbone said, clapping me on the back. "There's probably a *mail-trail* in every place you've frequented since birth! I would have brought them to the house, but my back isn't the iron-hinge it used to be. Sit down."

After indulging a few minutes in university gossip, Rathbone told me of his burgeoning relationship with Liz, my agent. He mentioned that we should double-date sometime, "that is if you can find a girl," Rathbone chortled, lighting a pipe. "Remember when you first came back from Alaska and had a hard time talking and being understood? Well, you should hear us, a Texan and an Englishman. We couldn't be further afield. But I guess opposites attract."

"Is it getting serious?" I inquired.

Rathbone nodded. "I asked her to move in with me. She said no, that we should be like Robert Browning and Elizabeth Barrett Browning. They were married, but lived in separate houses and dated, keeping their own identities. Saw each other at their best and kept it fresh."

"Might be something to that," I said.

"So tell me, how is the research going?"

I shook my head. "Socrates said it best: 'All I know is that I know nothing.' "

"Well, sounds to me like you're right on course."

"How so?"

"Every scientist hits that stretch where you feel lost, overwhelmed by the material, when none of the data makes any sense. I'd be worried if you *weren't* experiencing this for it means you truly are letting it all in, keeping an open mind, and not bending the data to fit a preconceived theorem." Rathbone paused to re-light his pipe. "Are you seeing anyone special?"

"There is this one woman, but I don't know…" I shrugged nonchalantly, holding back on talking about Ellen and her offer to go to Africa, knowing Rathbone would hound me to go.

Rathbone rocked back on his chair, exhaling a cloud of sweet smoke. "I'll tell you a story that my father once told me. There were two bulls in a pasture munching clover together with the cows in a separate field. One of the bulls was young, just coming into his prime; the other an old-timer, with grey hairs up around his horns. The young bull, feeling the urge, yanks his head up from the clover and says, 'Hey, old man, why don't we run over and hump a few*?'* The old bull just keeps on chewing; he finally lifts his head and says, 'No, son. Why don't we *walk* over and hump 'em ALL.' "

I sat there unimpressed.

Seeing that he was not getting through, Rathbone dropped his booming, professorial tone and leaned forward across his desk. "Be careful what you ask for, you just might get it."

"I *asked* for this?" I said, cocking my head to the side.

"Yes, you most certainly did. You set the wheels in motion. Years ago, sitting in that very chair, you said you wanted to study The Big Picture—and if memory serves me right—'Something with a heartbeat and emotions.' "

"Yes, and you sent me to Alaska."

"Which prepared you for what you now need to learn. And even I, a card-carrying member of the British Old Boys Club, know that it is women who are the stronger sex."

I nodded my head…indefatigable Ellen in my mind's eye still hovering orgasmically above the world. I stood and shook Rathbone's hand. As we walked toward the door, he placed an arm around my shoulders.

As if reading my mind, he said: "Men rule the world, but women rule the men and they do it primarily with a three-inch triangle between their legs. It's the center of the world. *Animus mundi.* Amazing, when you think about it…the hold they have on us."

I staggered out to the parking lot with a sack of mail slung over each shoulder like a stevedore toting heavy cargo or Prometheus bound. When I dropped my burdens into the trunk of the car, a few letters spilled out of one of the bags. A Columbia University envelope caught my eye. I grabbed it up and tore it open:

> *Dear Professor Mackenzie: I was wondering if you might please give me a call. I would like to ask for your guidance and possible participation in a research project in a field that you have great experience in. Thanks for your consideration.*
>
> *Most Sincerely,*
> *Lorelai Logan*
> *482-5672*

I punched in the number on my new cell phone. A young woman answered, thrilled to hear from me. She asked if I would mind meeting for coffee so she could explain her project? I readily agreed, eager to re-enter the realm of academia to talk of more down-to-earth, scientific matters for a change.

We decided to meet at *Cyberia*, a campus coffee house where, rather than conversing boisterously and passionately about politics, philosophy, films, and literature as I had remembered, solo students were tapping away silently on computers or thumbing tiny Blackberry keypads.

Moments after I sat down at a booth along the far wall, Lorelai Logan bounded in, dressed in ripped jeans, a Strokes concert t-shirt, and a navy blue baseball cap with brim backwards. In one smooth motion, she slid into the seat across from me as if she was stealing home. As she straightened up and I formally shook her hand, I couldn't help but notice that underneath the sporty garb, Ms. Logan possessed a fresh, newly-minted beauty: girl blooming just now into a woman.

As she leaned forward, twin curtains of glossy brown hair grazed the table-top and sparkling hazel eyes locked on to mine. She said that she was a junior majoring in biology; she loved my whale book and would like nothing more than to follow in my footsteps.

"But that's not really what I want to talk with you about."

"Oh?"

Without hesitation or self-consciousness (or coming up for air) Lorelai spoke: "As a sophomore, I took Dr. Fisher's class on *Human Sexuality* and got an Incomplete. I didn't finish my paper, which was seventy percent of the grade. My topic was *The Female Orgasm: Rock My World!* and I kept putting off the research because I was raised as a strict Catholic and sex before marriage is such a sin."

"The nuns hammered *THAT* into my brain only about a billion times," she rolled her eyes, "Ha! Like they should talk. The horny old crones told us over and over we weren't allowed to wear patent-leather shoes to the prom because the boys would look down to see up our skirts. And we should never be around white tablecloths because it reminds the boys of bed sheets, and when we go away to college and have a picture of a boyfriend on our desk we should turn the picture around when we undress—who even THINKS of that shit!

"One time my brother walked into our all-girls school early to give me a ride home and alarms went off and doors slammed shut. The whole place went into lockdown as if he was Attila the Hun."

She continued non-stop. "And one nun used to prowl around at dances, poking her cane in between us when we slow danced, screeching: 'Leave room for the Holy Spirit!' SICK! And *we* were supposed to be the ones hormonally crazed.

"It only stands to reason that I should know what the hell I'm doing… *Hello!* …before getting married. If I don't know my way *around the world* so to speak, my husband, who I already have picked out and he's quite a player…well, all that's going to change when he marries me and I rock his world and suck the Holy Ghost right out of him. And so as not to leave any loose ends on my college record *and* wanting to learn how to be a great lay before getting married…"

"…I was wondering with all your experience with the *Cosmo* girls—the best one for all-time in my book being Helen Gurley Brown, who even though she's older now will always be a Babe, the female Hugh Hefner, or Hefner is the male Helen Gurley Brown—thank God, liberating women from Puritanism and chauvinism and Catholicism and you must have acquired so much experience and knowledge by now about how a girl can please a guy and vice-versa…"

She didn't even take a breath before continuing. "… and since you no longer work here we wouldn't get into trouble if you were Hot Teacher and I wore my Catholic schoolgirl skirt and pig-tails and no underwear, if you want to go *old-school* on me. Or hey, I'll dress up as a nun with thigh-high stockings and pale white skin under my black habit if you like, for payback, because I heard somewhere you were raised Catholic, too. With our similar backgrounds and your current *Cosmo* knowledge—gawd how many girls have you had by now, you naughty boy? Well, who better to help me complete my Incomplete, but *YOU*?"

After my brain finally caught up to the end of her torrential pitch, I mumbled: "Men's room..." I wandered flushed and sweating across Cyberia. Inside the lavatory, desperate and seeing an open window, I climbed through (careful not to break anything with an uncontrollable erection swinging like a ball-peen hammer) dropped to the ground and dashed for the car, hunched over in a goose-walk with my hands held down across my tumescent front.

Once inside my apartment, I triple-locked the door and toppled onto the bed. Ever-dedicated to recording my findings while fresh, I opened the laptop on my beating chest and typed:

*THEOREM # 9: SUGAR SHOCK*

Don't know how much longer I can continue this study. I've tried to keep my distance emotionally, remain aloof and impersonal—keep control factors securely in place, but of all the animals I've studied, the human female is the most unpredictable, sexual, and uncontrollable in every way. I am putty in their hands (hell, don't even have to be that close for the wood to harden). I've never been this exhausted in my life. It's beyond kayaking-into-a-constant-headwind or mountain-climbing-vertical-walls tired. But why am I complaining? Before, I couldn't get laid for the life of me. Gawd, Lorelai Logan was drop-dead gorgeous, so fresh and delicious, and laid out right on the table for the taking, but I didn't even want a nibble (even though she tapped directly into my darkest fantasy: fucking a young, long-legged nun with hidden-away pale, white skin the color and taste of pastry). Why didn't I agree to put on the horn rims and play Hot Teacher? WHAT'S WRONG WITH ME?

Maybe it's because I feel stuffed, overloaded, like the only thing I've been eating for weeks is candy and now it's caught up with me. I'm in "sugar shock." Each woman has such a constant hunger and amazing, blazing energy that to really satisfy one would take an entire lifetime of full-time focus. I now want to go deeper, more into a woman's soul and try to satisfy THAT hunger for a change. (Skyler, especially, seems to get frustrated when we stay too much on the surface. She always wants to go deeper.) I know in the previous Theorem I extolled the virtues of variety, but I'm learning that to fully engage many women at once is damned hard work, a full-time job requiring supreme organizational skills, the sexual stamina of a bull ("Walk over and hump 'em ALL"—my ass), emotional denial, and very deep pockets. A man should have as many women as he can keep happy. In my case right now, that's none.

I'm seriously thinking of going off to Africa with Ellen. But... there's a strange dichotomy with her. The sex is so hot, but Ellen herself is not very warm.

# 21

## The Pieces Inside

I slept in the next morning, waking at ten, yet still feeling exhausted in a place deep down, at the core. I was in bed, sipping coffee, savoring the solitude and silence, when the phone rang. I let it go to the answering machine. I heard Skyler's calm, measured voice. "Michael, I just wanted to thank you for the wonderful time at the zoo. The way you explained everything, you made it all come alive."

I jumped up and grabbed the phone. "Thanks. I had a great time, too."

"Oh, good, you're there. The animals and plants were amazing! I've been reading how so many states are trying to replace evolution in the schools with religious doctrine. After seeing all that rich diversity at the zoo, I think Darwin got it right."

"Yeah. There's been life on Earth for four hundred million years. Think about how much happens during just one human lifetime. Multiply that by eons and the possibilities are endless."

"Speaking of how much happens in one life, if you're not busy tonight, or is that an oxymoron—*Cosmo* man *alone* when the sun goes down? Your dance card must be full for decades! If you want to take a break from it all, why don't you come over tonight? I make a killer shrimp and feta-cheese pizza."

Instead of cringing at the thought of more company, I suddenly felt re-energized knowing that with Skyler the pressure was off and all I had to do was just be myself.

"Yeah, be great to kick back."

I got dressed, and went out for something I had long been meaning to do. I walked into the Gotham Book Mart with Skyler's e-mail from Paris, the Reading List.

While finding the books on the list and stacking them in my arms, I was stopped mid-shelf by a familiar name, *Skyler Stevens*. No way. I set the other books down and flipped to the author photo on the back jacket flap. One and the same!

I sat down in an oversized chair with *Girl Nation*: documentary photos and interviews with girls and young women across the U.S. For most of the day, I saw and read about how from the time they are seven years old, girls are taught by mass-media that the only thing that makes them special is their sexuality.

A famous super model talked about her pictures in fashion magazines, "No one looks like that. I don't even look like that. Everything is airbrushed to impossible perfection."

In response to the question, "Would you rather be fat or dead?" Seventy-five percent of a thousand girls polled said *dead.* A well-muscled, world record holder from the Stanford University swim team commented: "When I don't wear makeup and am not near a mirror, I feel stronger because I live from within myself."

Back in my apartment, I showered, dressed, and carefully slid *Girl Nation* into my backpack.

As Skyler let me into her apartment, the first thing she asked was if I had started on the reading list she had sent me.

"I'm working on it," I said slowly, wondering if she was psychic or had seen me at the bookstore. "What should I read first?"

"*The Vagina Monologues.*"

"I didn't know it could talk."

We both laughed.

"Come on, your timing is perfect. Just took the pizza out of the oven."

We settled down at the table with the pizza and beers.

"Honestly, Michael, I don't know how you are keeping your sanity," Skyler said. "You should call that book you're writing about the *Cosmo* girls, *Heart Attack*."

"Yeah, that's exactly what it feels like most of the time. It looks great on the outside, but very confusing and exhausting working my way through it."

"Well, don't feel bad. The whole man-woman thing has perplexed poets and philosophers for centuries."

"You know what a lawyer said to me when I was in England doing interviews at the BBC?"

"What?"

"That he'd give me a blank check—fill in the amount, if I could get him in as the next *Cosmo* Bachelor."

"What did you say?"

"I quoted his countrymen, a certain band called The Beatles: *Money Can't Buy Me Love.* "

She smiled and served me another slice of pizza.

"Have you found anyone," she asked, "among the *Cosmo* outpouring that you feel serious about?"

"Yeah. There's this woman, Ellen. Been seeing her quite a bit. She's wealthy, and an anthropologist. She wants me to go to Africa with her soon for a scientific expedition. I don't know. What do you think I should do?"

Skyler pushed away her plate. "You should go. The worst sin is having regrets later in life. And hey…it's tough out there. If she can provide the funding and you both are compatible then you've—you've got it made."

Skyler got up and returned with coffee. Handing me a full mug, she asked, "Do you love her?"

I poured a dab of milk into my coffee and stirred slowly with a spoon. "Ellen doesn't believe in love."

"Let's go in the living room."

We sat in opposite chairs. "What about you?" I asked. "Have you ever been in love?"

"You mean true love?"

"Yes."

She shook her head. "I have very high standards."

"As in *impossibly* high?"

"Ever see the movie *Thelma and Louise*?"

"Yeah, even though it was a chick flick."

"Michael!"

I raised my hand. "*That* I learned a lot from."

"That's better. Well, when they are talking about men, Thelma tells Louise, 'You get what you settle for.' And I believe in only settling for the best, for true love. Don't believe in serial marriages, one after another. I want it once and I want it for the long haul. I want to share all the riches and tragedies of life and grow old together with just one man."

"Admirable. But what happens if you never meet him?"

"Then it's not meant to be. I'd rather have solo peace than the knotted tension and deceit that exist in a bad marriage. Hey," she said, pausing to sip her coffee, "there's something I want to ask you. From all your experiences, do you think it's better to make love one thousand times with one woman, or once with one thousand women?"

"Well, on Monday, Wednesday and Friday—I think it's better one thousand times with one, but then Tuesday, Thursday and Saturday—once with a thousand wins out."

Skyler set down her coffee cup and leaned forward. "What about Sundays? The tie-breaker."

I squirmed in my seat.

"You know," Skyler said. "I could understand men jumping from one woman to the next, if each had different equipment Each woman a totally *new* experience apparatus wise, but I just don't get the drive to have us all, when physically we're all the same."

"But you're not the same. Each woman makes the apparatus different."

"How so?"

"Awareness. When a woman has what men, ahem, call *ass awareness*, it's like her consciousness also extends down there, empowering her sex with an individual life of its own. For a man it's like discovering fire again for the very first time no matter how many times he's warmed himself before."

I sighed deeply. "I wish women could see themselves for one day through our eyes. How beautiful and beguiling and overpoweringly alluring you are to us. Then you might understand. To you, you're just everyday you. But to us, my God, that *otherness*... For a man, just to see the beauty of women is reason enough to be alive!"

Skyler smiled. "But why not feel that way about just one woman?"

I looked her directly in the eyes. "Believe me, I'm thinking about it. But I worry if you marry at one point in time, what's to prevent those same two people from changing over the next fifty years? The ancient Greek philosopher Heraclitus said: 'There is nothing permanent except change.' Also, I worry about not being able to control my DNA, override my programming."

"What?"

"Genetically men are hard-wired to be breeders. The biological drive to propagate the species doesn't care about man-made: love, marriage, fidelity. Don't mean to be crude, but that saying: *A stiff dick has no conscience* is true and it's not our fault. Men are programmed to be polygamous, sow our seeds far and wide for genetic diversity. And that's why evolution crafted the female form to be so sexualized, so we won't ever lose interest in Job One. So, I worry about staying faithful when I'm married, being life-long monogamous after the initial passion dies down and while sitting on the sideline, having Coach DNA shouting at me to get back in the game."

"An honest assessment, but who says the passion has to die down, big boy?" she said. "I think it was your Heraclitus who also said: 'You never step in the same river twice.' If a couple is really committed to growing and changing together, sex can be that different each time."

"Really?"

"Yes. Just the other day, I was reading a magazine article about long-term relationships—marriages that have stood the test of time and the great novelist Gabriel García Márquez said that his wife has become so familiar to him that he doesn't know her anymore. As close as I am to my man, I will always be unknowable, a new challenge ongoing."

I shifted gears and asked Skyler about her past.

"When I was a girl, my Dad died of a heart attack in the arms of his mistress, then a year later my Mom died of breast cancer and a broken heart," she said. "Most of my life I've had to fend for myself. But I enjoy my job as a flight attendant; it pays well enough and lets me see the world." She paused. "So when are you leaving for Africa?"

I glanced over at her Christmas tree in the corner. "Soon. New Year's Eve."

"Can I ask a favor?"

"Sure."

She stood, found a pen, and picked up my book. She motioned me over to the couch, next to her. "Would you sign it for me?"

Bounding over and sitting down, my momentum pressed me against her. We both looked startled and slid slightly apart. She handed over the pen, but before giving me the book, she held it tight between her hands. "After reading this all the way through, I now know that I misjudged you that first time we went out and I stormed out of the restaurant."

"Well, some of what you said was true."

"Michael, what I'm trying to say is that you have a shot at being a real man. I was impressed." She shook the book. "You have reverence. You didn't try to conquer everything like most men do in nature. You learned and lived feminine principles—harmonizing with the world, and nurtured inner and outer resources. Men tend to treat women as they do the earth. I've seen it in my travels."

"In the Amazon where the rain forest is now being raped wholesale, women are treated like third class citizens. In parts of Africa, women are reduced to being laborious beasts of burden. They carry sixty to eighty pounds of firewood while men sleep the day away drunk under a shade tree, getting up to slaughter elephants for their ivory." But in Scandinavia: Norway, Sweden, Denmark, and Finland where men revere nature, women were first to hold the highest political offices in the land.

"I've seen the correlation in place after place," she said softly. "It is impossible for men to both honor women and at the same time, disrespect the earth. No coincidence that the Environmental and Feminist movements started at the very same time. And you lived the good parts of that in Alaska."

She handed me my book. I inscribed: *To Skyler Stevens, Fellow author and photographer. Your Friend, Michael Mackenzie.*

When she read it, her eyes widened, "How did you know?"

I unzipped my backpack and pulled out *Girl Nation.* "Found it without even looking. Sat all day in the bookstore reading it. I've learned so much about girls and women from this book. Sad in many ways."

She shrugged. "My small part in trying to show that females should judge themselves by what they have within, and not by shallow surface appearances. With reality stars and messed up actresses getting all the attention in the media and held up as role models, that's the end of civilization as we know it." A grin then softened her features. "Besides, you are a part of *Girl Nation.*"

"What?"

"I heard that you were in *Mister Sister* and even dressed the part."

"No way!"

"Don't worry. Your secret's safe with me." She patted my knee. "But it was interesting, to say the least, hearing about *Nanook of the North* in a silk peignoir."

"I was there, went undercover that night to try to see things from the feminine perspective. It was very enlightening. Every man should do it—once. Hope you don't think I'm weird or anything."

"No. I admire you even more. It takes a real man to be a woman."

"That's exactly what Suki said."

"The woman you went with?"

I nodded. "Hey, who told you?"

"One of the women in my book is a lesbian. We've stayed in touch and go out together occasionally; Linda was there that night and saw you."

"Are you lesbian or bi?"

She waggled her head side-to-side a la Mae West, "'I used to be Snow White, but I drifted.' "

I cracked up.

"I'm not bi or lesbian, but…"

"Not that there's anything wrong with it!" we both chorused the line from the *Seinfeld Show* re-runs. We laughed, shaking our heads over our synchronicity.

She grabbed the pen and signed her book: *To Michael Mackenzie, A man in touch with his feminine side. Your Friend, Skyler Stevens.*"

"Thanks. Are you still taking pictures?"

"All the time, but I'll never give up my day job. Being a flight attendant gives me security and health insurance, and my ticket to travel to the places and things I want to photograph."

"Are you working on anything now?"

"A book on sacred places around the world. Happiness comes from within, but what a person has within matters very little in our superficial society. What feeds the spirit is nature and simplicity. I'm trying to show that in the new book."

"I'm sure you'll succeed. Hey, can I ask you something?"

"Sure."

"I know it's the million dollar question, but what do women really want?"

"In a man?"

"Yes."

She sighed and set down her coffee. "Everything. Not every thing, but for a man to try to develop every quality within, even the things that seem threatening or opposed, that you think wouldn't match, but do, creating a balanced, complete—a vast man with no borders or limits to his growth. Like a kaleidoscope, dazzling a woman by having all the pieces inside, but arranged differently, when need be, at different times.

Above all, a man who's not afraid to show that inside the steel armor there beats a fragile heart. A man who is both strong..."

Suddenly we were staring into one another's eyes, and we leaned in closer, eyes locked together.

"And tender..."

Our lips touched and we both sprang back, as if from an electrical shock.

"Sorry!" I said, leaping to my feet.

Skyler shook her head as if breaking a spell. "Yes, right—*well,*" she said, head down, hands smoothing her skirt.

I strode toward the door. "I'll keep in touch. I don't think I can call or e-mail from where we'll be in Africa, but there's always snail…"

"Michael."

"What?"

"Good luck," Skyler said, followed by a feeble wave of her hand.

# 22

# Owned This Song

I called Rathbone at the university and informed him of my decision to go to Africa with Ellen.

He was thrilled, going on and on about the exotic magic of Madagascar and its many endemic species. He ended his enthusiastic response with, "And when do I get to meet her?"

"Friday night, if you can please take me to the airport?"

"My pleasure. And what an opportunity. If you find that aquatic dinosaur, you'll make history!"

"Can I meet you and the guys after class today? Let's close down Mission Control and have a farewell drink together. Tell Ralph he can sublet the apartment again if he wants."

Later that day, Rathbone, the TAs, and I rolled into Rathbone's house, waving bottles of Scotch, presents, and medical supplies.

Kwame high-fived me. "AF-*REE*-KA! Homey, you done me proud. You be a brother in no time!" He presented me with a green and gold dashiki with a matching round cap. I put them on and hugged him with gratitude.

"Dude, darken down about ten shades and you might pass," Ralph smirked.

"So, tell us about the girl," Steve inquired. "She must really be something!"

"She's all right," I shrugged.

They all nodded knowingly and exchanged smiles: minimalist verbiage between men, all it takes to describe a woman perfectly.

"Is she a *Cosmo* girl?" Steve asked.

"Yeah. At least she said she wrote in," I said.

"Well, let's find out," Ralph said. "Time to close up shop, anyway."

Entering Mission Control, we stopped and looked around the room like dazed treasure seekers surrounded by El Dorado.

"Hey, remember Shareen?" Rathbone said, pointing to her picture on the wall. "Your first date, the body double. I do think I saw a close-up of her derrière in the new Sharon Stone movie."

"Derrière? Man, Dean R, that's beyond old-school," Kwame dissed. "Nobody says the word derrière. It's booty, baby, boo-*tay!*"

Ralph seated himself in front of the computer. "You wanna see who the computer thinks, out of all the *Cosmo* girls, is your perfect match? I programmed it from the beginning to give its final choice once all the data was entered."

"What kind of odds are we talking about?" Steve said. "How many girls are in there?"

Ralph rapped some keys. "Currently there are 12,594 entries. Ready, dude? Ready to see who the computer picks as your one-and-only?"

We all huddled together tightly around the screen. I took a slug of scotch and bottle in hand flung my arms around my buddies. "Let 'er rip, mateys."

Ralph hit a three-key sequence and the computer screen went dark. "It's concentrating," Ralph said. A long minute passed as the computer made groaning sounds... "There are a ton of girls on its hard drive."

"See, even the 'puter can't pick just one!" Steve said.

Finally, the screen brightened and a very impressive set of credentials scrolled forth, followed by a photo of *Ellen Klein*, 112 Park Avenue, New York, NY.

"WOW!" Rathbone and the TAs all chorused.

Ralph rapped some more keys to examine the back-code. "I've never seen so many variables link up. She," Ralph tapped the screen, "is definitely the one for you."

"Is it a match?" Kwame said. "She the one you going off to Africa with?"

With a trembling hand, I lifted the bottle of Scotch and took a long pull.

"He'll tell us when he's ready," Rathbone announced, glancing at me. "Come on, let's go out and celebrate, whoever the choice!"

"Yeah!" Ralph said, shutting down the computer.

"Hair of the dog," Steve chortled.

"*Woof. Wooof.*" Kwame barked.

We all charged out the door and went to a nearby karaoke bar. We drank and laughed and discussed women, sports, and future plans. Ralph swiveled around to cast a glance at a horrid performance of *Achy, Breaky Heart.* "Scary-oke," Ralph said.

"Hey, a toast," Steve said. "May all your ups and downs in life be between the sheets!"

We clinked glasses. Seeing that I was quiet, the TAs and Rathbone carried the conversation. While they were engrossed in a good-natured argument about the recent World Series, I tossed back my Scotch and slammed the glass down. As if pushed by an invisible force, I jumped up from the table, trotted onto the stage, grabbed the open mike, and gave my request to the karaoke attendant. I closed my eyes to focus, then began:

*"To all the girls I've loved before*
*Who traveled in and out my door*
*I'm glad they came along*
*I dedicate this song*
*To all the girls I've loved before*

*"To all the girls I once caressed*
*And may I say I've held the best*
*For helping me to grow*
*I owe a lot I know*
*To all the girls I've loved before."*

I was so sincere and overflowing with experiences from my heart that immediately the song transformed from a goof to a cathartic prayer. I owned this song. I sang the hell out of it with a voice I didn't know I had. The effect upon the room was electric. The raucous, drunken crowd fell silent and turned to the stage.

*"To all the girls who cared for me*
*Who filled my nights with ecstasy*
*They live within my heart*
*I'll always be a part*
*Of all the girls I've loved before."*

On the memory screen behind my eyes, the women I'd met paraded by as I sang. I saw Shareen coming out of the bathroom in her tool belt... Miss Memphis bursting into tears in bed... Snogging a surprised Doctor Devi...Vivi Correa's dazzling, full-feathered samba around my living room... Dressed as a woman and walking into Mister Sister with Suki... Skyler, the Sky-Goddess, in her uniform... Ellen, wearing only a wicked grin, sitting back in a chair, rolling golden Ben Wa balls in her hand... Lorelai, the sex-crazed coed talking rapid-fire in Cyberia... The *Bitches & Ho's* at Halloween…The unknown babe who reached up to straighten my *spooren* at Bid for Bachelors.

*"To all the girls I once caressed*
*And may I say I've held the best*
*For helping me to grow*
*I owe a lot I know*
*To all the girls I've loved before*

*"The winds of change are always blowing*
*And every time I try to stay*
*The winds of change continue blowing*
*And they just carry me away..."*

The crowd gave a standing ovation. With the applause cutting into my delirium—I dashed off stage to the Men's room, entered a stall, slammed the metal door shut, bowed my head—and sobbed.

# 23

# The Flame of the Forest

The next evening, I took a cab with three big suitcases to Rathbone's house, ready to leave for Africa. Walking in the door, I saw Steve.

"You're here?" I said, surprised.

"Yeah, figured I'd finish sealing up the boxes, but it's a slow go. I keep looking at the pictures and re-reading the letters. Where do you want to keep all of this?"

"Rathbone is storing it here."

"Good thing he has a big house."

"Can I ask you something?"

"Sure."

"You've been the one most interested in the women. How come?"

"Because I'm married. You have what I don't and you have it in great and varied profusion. It's like I've been on a contact high, living vicariously through you these last few weeks. Can't remember when I've felt so alive!"

"Yeah, but you have what I don't: a wife, kid—the stability of a family."

"It's a trade-off."

"How so?"

"When married, you trade passion for comfort."

I let this soak in. "How long have you been hitched?"

"Seven years."

"You miss the passion?"

Steve nodded. "I love my wife, but what I would give for just one more night of red hot, super-soaker sex, when that animal rush goes through you like, *THIS* IS WHAT IT

MEANS TO BE *ALIVE!* Marriage works against passion. There's the stress of bills, dealing with the daily nitty-gritty, not seeing each other at your best. You become habituated to each other and the heat is gone."

"You know," he continued, glancing around the room. "I've got a confession to make. I've been bringing this excitement home to the wife. There's been a big increase in the frequency and heat in our physical relations. I think that's why she didn't mind me being over here as long as you were the only one actually dating the women."

"Whoa. Well, thanks for the honesty. It's like sex influences everything."

Steve nodded. "I just read in a dual biography of Einstein and Picasso how every time they made a major scientific discovery or painting style, it was at the same time they had a new mistress."

"Woman as muse."

"Yes," Steve continued, "spikes in their libido launched quantum leaps, major advances in art and science. Hemingway, too. Every novel was inspired by a new woman. So, yes, sex is important and influential. But society is set up to repress it. Domesticity makes a man docile. Before pitching in over here, I was getting soft, fat, losing my edge." He looked around wistfully. "I'm going to miss this."

"You sound like Ellen. She says that trying to contain the sex drive is like trying to fit a tornado into a teacup."

"Sounds like she totally understands. Wait a minute... The same Ellen the computer picked is *your* Ellen?"

I nodded.

"Damn!" Steve slapped his thigh. "What are the odds of that?"

"Still can't believe it."

"Wow. Congratulations! That's awesome. But hey, don't get me wrong. Marriage has many benefits. I just miss the wild life, that's all."

We were taping the last of the boxes when Rathbone came in. Seeing the mountain stacked up, he whistled. He tried to pick up a box, but it wouldn't budge. "You can judge your popularity by the pound! A ton of love here, at least."

"What time is your plane?" Steve asked.

I glanced at my watch. "Wow. Soon."

Steve helped carry my suitcases down to Rathbone's car. I thanked him for everything and we bro-hugged.

"Something you said to me when I first came back," I said, "I now say to you, in parting."

"What's that?" Steve said.

"'Keep it wild.'"

He laughed. As the car pulled away, he stood in the street hopping up and down and thumping his chest with his fists.

Arriving at the airport, Rathbone left the car in the short term parking lot. I checked my bags, and we walked together to the gate. When Rathbone was introduced to Ellen, his craggy eyebrows shot up as he recognized her as the computer's pick. As Rathbone and I hugged goodbye, he whispered in my ear, "You sure know how to pick a winner."

As we settled in to wait to board the flight, Ellen sensed that something was troubling me. She said that I seemed distant, not all there. "Is Mr. Bachelor sad about leaving all his girls behind?" she asked.

"No," I shrugged.

"Well, I've got to check on some instruments, delicate archeology scales and picks—make sure they're handed-carried down to cargo." She looked around, took my arm, and pulled me behind a tall pillar. With both hands she reached up under her skirt and in one smooth move slid her panties down and stepped out of them. She handed them to me. "This will keep you company. Be right back," she grinned.

As I watched her walk away, the black satin flowed like syrup through my fingers. I lifted it to my nose and sniffed. I slipped her panties into my pants pocket and took a seat in the lounge.

While waiting in the boarding area, an airport attendant rolled in an elderly woman in a wheelchair. I recognized Evangeline, from the flight to London. She had been with her husband Fred and they were so much in love, even after all those years together. I walked over to her and re-introduced myself, reminding her about being on the same flight.

"Oh, yes!" Evangeline brightened.

"Great to see you. How have you been? Where's Fred?"

"Oh, Michael..."

I guessed from her expression that Fred had died. I took her hand. "I'm sorry."

Evangeline looked up at me. "Don't be. I miss him terribly, but have no regrets—not a one. I was so blessed to have sixty-five years with that man and we lived and loved each and every day, in every way. Michael—we were such friends, the very best of friends all life long!"

I couldn't take my eyes from hers. Flashing back over their life together, Evangeline's eyes sparkled like multi-faceted diamonds. She looked at me as if staring directly into my soul. "Of course you can love more than one woman at the same time. But by committing to someone fully—pouring all your love into one person—building a life together hour by hour, day by day, the richness you share and the depths you go are worth more than anything on..."

She turned away, her eyes glittering with a wealth of memories. I squeezed her hand, bent down to kiss her cheek, and left her to her thoughts.

I walked over to a seat facing the runway. In the dark glass I saw my reflection. My eyes glistened as rain streaked the windows. *I'm running away...*

As the passengers were called to board the plane, Ellen returned out of breath. "The stupid fucking idiots! They sent the instruments down on the conveyor belt. Fuckers! I told them over and over..."

As Ellen continued her rant, I suddenly saw past her surface beauty to her cold spirit inside. I reached into my pocket and pulled out the only thing that had ever really held us together. I handed her panties back. "Sorry. I can't go."

I walked away—leaving her standing, open-mouthed, at the gate.

Outside the airport after reclaiming my bags, I hailed a cab. From the back seat, I called Rathbone on my cell phone.

"Plane delayed?" But before I could answer, Rathbone gushed: "Ellen is everything the computer said and more!"

I said, "The plane has left and obviously, I'm not on it."

"Oh. Ah, cold feet. Understandable. You hardly had time to get to know her. Take a day or two—believe me, she is perfect for you and it's not too late. Call her and say you're coming over in a few days."

After repeated coaxing from Rathbone to go to the faculty New Year's Eve party that night, I finally vocalized my feelings. "You can't choose a woman by computer! Love can't be reduced down to bits and bytes. It's a travesty to do so or to think you can study women scientifically. Women haven't bought into the overly-rational, the scientific—they know intuitively that only snuffs the magic. We need to return to when goddesses ruled the earth!"

There was an audible sucking in of air—then Rathbone said, "You're not in your right mind. Come to the party. Best thing for you. Bring in the New Year with your cronies."

"Thank you for everything and Happy New Year," I said, flipping the phone shut.

Seeing Central Park come into view out the cab window, I abruptly asked the driver to stop, then paid him extra to take my bags on to my apartment and leave them in the foyer. I walked alongside the zoo. A wind moved through the trees. As I watched the leaves shake, again I heard the tintinnabulation of tiny bells and Dzunukwa's laughter. I followed a tight swirl of leaves at my feet as they blew through the open entrance gate.

I saw a sign, WELCOME ZOOLOGICAL SOCIETY AND ALL ANIMAL LOVERS TO THE NEW YEAR'S EVE PARTY! I slipped past the chatter and music in the main administration building and entered The Rare Plants Conservatory, the ceiling a curved-glass dome. As I turned my head looking for a particular plant, a beam of moonlight guided my eyes. I followed the radiance, then stopped. Looking down, my eyes widened. Hearing someone approaching, I stepped behind the tall, bushy plant.

Arriving at the same plant, a hooded figure halted. The hood was lowered and I heard a gasp. Upraised in the center of the Flame of the Forest, in the final hour of the last night of the year, a brilliant red flower was in full bloom.

I stepped out of the jungle and into Skyler's astonished embrace.

# 24

# Home

With a rustle of large wings, an eagle lifted off from my leather-sleeved arm and circled a familiar Alaskan island. Standing on a high promontory with Skyler, I took her hand. We kissed tenderly, then passionately.

Back at the cabin, I chopped wood, my face split into a constant smile all the while, in awe that I could be this happy. I had it *all* with Skyler: friendship and sex, body and soul, sass and harmony. She was the complete package—intelligent, beautiful, and a feminine feminist. I shook my head over how she had been there the entire time, hidden in plain sight. As I swung the axe in a productive rhythm, I recalled what Sherlock Holmes had once told Watson: "If you want to hide something, don't bury it in the ground, but place it out on the mantle in full view, for we are blind to what's right in front of us."

Having previously discounted Skyler as *just a friend*, I now realized that friendship was the most important part of compatibility. Spike friendship with passion and I now felt complete. I vowed to be constantly romantic, never take her for granted, and most of all, make her happiness essential to my own.

As I watched a flock of geese winging gracefully overhead, gabbling in high-note tones, I was grateful to all the *Cosmo* women for everything they had taught me—that I would now put into practice with Skyler. *The riches they gave me—the honesty, wild eroticism, and stunning femininity—goddesses, each and all.*

Skyler came out of the cabin wearing my parka—holding the Victoria's Secret model picture she'd found tacked up on a wall. She shook it questioningly in front of me. I blushed and stammered. She dropped the page, threw open the parka, and smiled. She was wearing the very same lingerie. She pounced on me like a hungry cat.

After sleeping for ten hours, dead to the world inside the cozy cabin, I awoke feeling reborn. Seeing that light in her eyes when she looked at me…my God, *that* was the greatest honor a man could have in this world! I vowed to live a life worthy of that look. Hearing my stomach rumble with hunger, I slipped out of bed and took the kilt down from a hook on the wall, reverently wrapping the warm field of ancestral wool around my waist.

I carefully opened the creaky cabin door and stepped outside. I walked into the forest, and filled a bowl with wild strawberries, wet with dew and warmed by the sun.

Back inside the cabin, I made strong coffee and strawberry pancakes on a cast-iron griddle atop the crackling wood stove; I took a tray to the back of the cabin and served Skyler breakfast in bed.

After a long, grateful kiss, she said, "It's so quiet, I can hear my heart."

"I can hear it, too."

She sat up bare-breasted, her wavy blond hair relaxed and natural like spun gold around her beautiful face; she was fresh off the brush of Botticelli—*The Birth of Venus.*

I couldn't eat, so filled was I by her. As we made love, for the first time in my life, I knew I was home.

Later that afternoon, the reflections of the surrounding forest and snow-flecked mountains were painted on the calm surface of the bay. Skyler was outside on the beach. She interlaced her fingers, raised her arms, arched her back and stretched up onto tiptoes, inhaling deeply a mix of ocean iodine and the sweet tang of forest cedar wood as if filling her being.

We carried two kayaks down to the edge of the sea. I handed her a strange piece of outerwear and took up my own. I held the circular garment down by my legs, stepped in; pulled the straps up over my shoulders and yanked down on the rubber hoop so it encircled my waist. She burst into laughter. "A kilt on a man I like, but a spray skirt? Michael, you look like a giant mushroom!"

"Yeah, yeah. You laugh, but let a 38-degree ocean wave fall into your unprotected lap and we'll see who's laughing then."

"I'm just kidding."

"I know, babe. But I want you to take this place seriously. Alaska will seduce you with beauty and the next minute try to kill you."

Once comfortably seated in our kayaks, spray skirts snugly attached around the cockpit rims, we pushed off the beach and paddled out into the bay. Rounding a distant point, Skyler gasped. Rimming the distant shore was an immense ice mass, thirty stories tall and a mile wide. Across its entire face, in crenulated folds and recessed hollows, the glacier glittered with electric-blue light. We paddled in closer; she lifted her camera and zoom lens, shooting high and low.

There were deep, thunder-like rumblings and tall ice towers collapsed across the face—falling into the ocean as if in slow motion.

"My God, it's stunning!" Skyler said.

We slowly flicked our paddles, moving through the ice field composed of various-sized bergs that had calved off the glacier face. We stopped paddling and drifted as I pointed out a crystal bird afloat on the water... a cut-glass flower atop a long stem... a rabbit in full-stride.

"Some days, it's as if the ice imitates the animate world," I said.

A massive white iceberg as big as an island hove into view. "Careful, give it a wide berth. Most of it is underwater."

"It's huge! Can we get out and stretch our legs on that one?"

"Not a good idea. As big as it is, it'll roll over or break apart at any moment. The salt-water is eating away at it from underneath in the fissures and cracks."

As we swung wide around the ice island, directly before us was a large heart, propped upright and glowing with topaz blue light.

"WOW! Look at *THAT!*" she exclaimed, camera lifting. "My favorite one. Look at that *color!* So blue—yet it's translucent, you can see right through it."

"It's called *heart ice.* From the deep center or heart of the glacier. For centuries, the glacier's crushing weight and pressure pushed down on it, squeezing out all the air bubbles and snow, so all that's left is ice in its purest form. But this is amazing," I marveled. "I've never seen it actually form the shape of what it's called."

As we drew closer, the big heart suddenly shattered into many pieces. We watched in stunned silence as the ice shards fell to the surface and floated away—bumping against our boats.

"Michael."

"Yeah?"

"If you ever do that to me, I'll never forgive you."

I gulped, and paddled hard through the shards. "Skyler, all I know is that right now, if you stacked up all the ice in Alaska it wouldn't reach half as high as the love I feel for you. I am so hot for you."

"How hot?"

"This hot." I did an Eskimo roll—driving my right shoulder down into the icy water and dropping until I was upside down. The cold was so shocking it nearly made me scream. But I kept my mouth shut and teeth clenched and moved the paddle in a frenzied figure-eight sculling motion. I finally rolled through the water with enough force to pop upright—back to life.

"MICHAEL! I WAS SO…"

"This hot, baby. This. Smokin'. Hot."

"Omigod—you're *STEAMING!*"

I put my head back and shouted: "I'M SKY-HIGH IN LOVE WITH SKYLER! *WAA-HOOOOooooooo!!*"

My exaltation sped through the crystal-clear air, rocketed up over the glacier, bounced off the granite cliffs, and echoed back down around us.

"I want closer..." She jabbed the ocean with the paddle and glided right up alongside me. "That's better," she grinned, leaning over to rub her cold nose against mine. I shook my head laughing, and reached forward and back, threading my lines through her kayak's tow holes—rafting us together.

We kissed and drifted aimlessly in the ice field, becalmed, without a care in the world. The air was fresh and pure. "Champagne air," I said to Skyler. "You can get giddy just breathing the oxygen here." All around us small ice chunks clicked and popped in the sunshine. The weather was *severe clear*, what pilots call infinite visibility.

*Is it because of the high-pressure weather or because I'm in love that I can see every pine needle on every distant tree?* I wondered.

Skyler said that besides being love-drunk with me, she felt totally saturated by Alaska, her senses processing so many new sights and sounds she felt keened to a high level of excitement. Even though we were hyper-aware of the vast surroundings, we were totally absorbed in each other—there was no distinguishing between the two. Out in that wild, remote amphitheater, we were the world and the world was two kids crazy in love.

A piercing cry broke our kiss.

"Chak?" she asked dreamily, gazing upward.

I squinted. "Looks like him. Same wing profile."

"Look at him *go!*"

We watched the eagle effortlessly riding the wind. Then Chak was no longer alone as another eagle soared in and the two of them brushed wingtips and lifted together high, higher in tightening gyres.

We kissed again, finding such heat and sweet succor at each other's core. She reached over and abruptly tugged the release tab on my spray skirt. Her eyes widened and she rolled a shoulder: "Is that an oosik under your spray skirt or ya happy ta see me?" We laughed and laughed. Even the icebergs around us matched our joy—glowing radiant gold in the setting sun.

Suddenly a leaden crunch shook us from our bliss. "The Loch Ness monster," she whispered in my ear.

Overtaking us, nearly the length of the kayaks, was a perfectly-formed sea monster complete with long tapered neck topped by a protruding head. I popped the hatch cover behind me and took out extra rope. I tied one end around both our cockpit rims; made a loop in the other end—and flung the lasso around the neck of ice.

"Now, where were we?"

The sea serpent bucked up and down in a flood tide, towing the lovers home.

Deep in the center of the island, the wind blew. The trees danced. Dzunukwa's wooden arms lifted and red flowers bloomed across the land.

## Skyler Stevens-Mackenzie

**Species Name:** *Skylark Feminista*
**Habitat & Range:** Everywhere, but not easily seen by the male due to distractions from
flashier and more aggressive females.
**Identifying Characteristics:** Independent, intelligent, and wildly imaginative practitioner in the erotic arts.
**Best Known For:** Monogamous breeder, mates for life (and inspires the male to do so). After pair-bonding, as parents, they show pride and joy in raising their chicks. In this case, two girls, who along with their mother, continue to delight and instruct the male with their natural beauty and wisdom.